HITLER'S
HENCHMEN

HITLER'S HENCHMEN

NAZI EXECUTIONERS AND HOW THEY ESCAPED JUSTICE AFTER WWII

HELMUT ORTNER
TRANSLATED BY GRAHAM HARRIS

FRONTLINE
BOOKS

First published in Great Britain in 2022 by
FRONTLINE BOOKS
an imprint of Pen & Sword Books Ltd,
47 Church Street, Barnsley, S. Yorkshire, S70 2AS

ISBN: 978-1-52679-110-8

CIP data records for this title are available from the British Library

For more information on our books, please visit
www.frontline-books.com, email info@frontline-books.com
or write to us at the above address.

Printed and bound by CPI Group (UK) Ltd, Croydon, CR0 4YY
Typeset by Concept, Huddersfield, West Yorkshire

Pen & Sword Books Limited incorporates the imprints of Atlas, Archaeology,
Aviation, Discovery, Family History, Fiction, History, Maritime, Military,
Military Classics, Politics, Select, Transport, True Crime, Air World,
Frontline Publishing, Leo Cooper, Remember When, Seaforth Publishing,
The Praetorian Press, Wharncliffe Local History, Wharncliffe Transport,
Wharncliffe True Crime, White Owl and After the Battle.

For a complete list of Pen and Sword titles please contact
PEN & SWORD LTD
47 Church Street, Barnsley, South Yorkshire, S70 2AS, England
E-mail: enquiries@pen-and-sword.co.uk

Or

PEN AND SWORD BOOKS
1950 Lawrence Rd, Havertown, PA 19083, USA
E-mail: Uspen-and-sword@casematepublishers.com

The German perpetrator was not a special German. What we have to say here about his morality does not apply to him in particular, but towards Germany as a whole.

Raul Hilberg

CONTENTS

THE PAST IN THE PRESENT
OR: MR HANNING ON TRIAL

In Detmold, Westphalia, a trial that had attracted worldwide attention came to an end in June 2016. In the dock was a 94-year-old man: the former Auschwitz SS guard Reinhold Hanning. Although the judges could not prove his direct involvement in the crime, he was sentenced to five years in prison on at least 170,000 counts of being an accessory to murder. An unusual verdict. During the trial, Hanning did what most of his generation had done for the last seventy years when it came to what they did and did not do between 1933 and 1945: he remained silent.

He did not even tell his family about Auschwitz, his defense lawyer reported. Hanning's grown-up son sat in the back of the courtroom: perplexed, speechless, unsure. What did he know about his father's actions? What could he have known? Had he ever asked him about Hitler's Germany, about Auschwitz, about his time as a young soldier? Silence often involves two people: one who says nothing and another who asks nothing. After the war, many German families remained silent.

"You were in Auschwitz for almost two and a half years and thus promoted mass murder," said Judge Anke Grudda at the beginning of the verdict. The public prosecutor's office had initially demanded a six-year prison sentence, seeing it as a proven fact that the former death camp guard and his unit had contributed to the functioning of the murder machine at Auschwitz.

Hanning was deployed to Auschwitz from 1943 to 1944, and during the trial had admitted to having been a member of the SS at the Nazi death camp and to having known about the mass murder that took place there. The defense had asked for an acquittal. In its view, no evidence of its client's direct involvement in the murders had been presented at the trial. At no point did he kill or help to kill anyone. He had only done his duty as a guard.

In a statement, Hanning had expressed remorse about his SS membership. "I am ashamed that I saw injustice happen before my eyes and did nothing to stop it." He wished he had never been to the concentration camp.

It was clear he was being sincere, but the court still had doubts. There was "no opportunity to know the real Reinhold Hanning," the judge stated soberly. The joint plaintiffs were certainly not convinced by the former SS man's sincere remorse.

Hanning had contributed to the "smooth running of mass extermination" and had accepted the killings without question. According to the court, how great his contribution was to such matters was unimportant. He was there, and that made him guilty. Judge Anke Grudda spoke directly to the 94-year-old, who was sitting in a wheelchair and hardly moved as her words sank in: "For two and a half years you watched people being murdered in gas chambers. For two and a half years you watched people being shot. For two and a half years you watched people starve to death."

Hanning had accepted his work, had been promoted twice in Auschwitz and had not allowed himself to be transferred to the front. According to the judge, the fact he did not want to work on the ramp, where people were sorted for work and the rest were sent directly to the gas chamber, was just a way of protecting himself. What's more, she expressed serious doubts about this: "We think it's completely absurd that you never stood on the ramp." Likewise, it is "impossible that not once did you see how people went to the gas chambers." The old man looked down. There was silence in the courtroom.

Grudda spoke for an hour. Afterwards, the prosecutor said that her words marked "a milestone in the reappraisal of Nazi injustice in Germany". The co-prosecutor said it was the first time a German court had heard that every SS man at Auschwitz shared the collective responsibility for all the murders that took place there. In fact, this guilty verdict was a message: as an SS member in Auschwitz, everyone had become a perpetrator. "The entire camp resembled a factory designed to kill people," the judge said.

"You weren't allowed not to participate at Auschwitz."

After the trial, many questions remained unanswered. Can the law still punish someone for a crime committed more than seventy years earlier? Can a court adequately punish someone for participating in the Holocaust? And what about the victims? Can they have any justice at all? Finally, there was one question that hovered over the entire trial: Why did it take more than seven decades for the accused to be tried?

The answer is as simple as it is terrifying. Because society, the State, the courts, did not want it. Not after the war, not in the Adenauer Republic, not in the social democratic Brandt-Schmidt era, not under Helmut Kohl (who liked to speak – misleadingly enough – of the "grace of late birth"), not even in the red-green government period (in which, after all, numerous commissions were set up to investigate Nazi involvement and personnel continuities in the ministries) in the past years of the grand coalition of the CDU and SPD.

One does not want to hold governments directly accountable for responsible public prosecutor's offices' and the authorities' lack of interest, as well as the delay in the proceedings, but there was a consistent lack of legislative direction throughout. There was a lack of *will* to bring Nazi perpetrators to justice before they became too old.

"This trial is the least a society can do to bring some justice to Holocaust survivors," said Anke Grudda, chair of the Assize court. The case was a warning of the courts' failures towards today's generation.

Thus, the criminal proceedings against Reinhold Hanning remain primarily a symbol. A reminder that participation in state mass murders must not go unpunished, even if this only happens many decades later.

Hanning, the former SS guard, was convicted at the age of 94. It is unlikely there will be any other similar trials, which also makes Reinhold Hanning a symbolic figure: his guilty verdict is a reminder that tens of thousands of murderers, desk clerks and accomplices to murder got away.

It should be noted that the reappraisal of Nazi injustice by German post-war courts is a story of delay followed by delay. The judiciary has fundamentally failed, and it is a shameful failure.

Here are some figures: from 1945 to 2005, a total of 172,294 people were investigated for criminal acts carried out during the Nazi era in the three western zones and the Federal Republic of Germany. This is only a tiny fraction given the monstrous crimes and the number of people involved. There were reasons for this: in the beginning, the same people who sat on the courts were the same ones who had done so during the Nazi era, with many reluctant to set to work. There was also political pressure to put an end to such proceedings, and countless amnesty laws ensured this was done.

Ultimately, only 16,740 cases resulted in indictments – and only 14,693 of the accused had to testify in court. In the end, just 6,656 people were convicted, with 5,184 being acquitted, often for lack of evidence. Most of the convictions – around 60 percent – ended with short prison sentences of up to one year. Just 9 percent of all prison sentences were higher than five years.

Against the backdrop of one of the greatest crimes in human history, this is a scandalous, outrageous record.

The Nazi perpetrators had nothing to fear from the courts, but what about from society, acquaintances, neighbors, or employers? "God, there has to be an end at some point," was the unanimous view, in the spirit of post-war Chancellor Adenauer, who, in October 1952, warned the SPD member of parliament Fritz Erler in the Bundestag that one should finally put an end to "Nazi hunting" because "once you start, it's hard to know where it ends".

With that, Adenauer articulated the zeitgeist of the post-war years. Most Germans no longer wanted to hear about war criminals, about crimes against humanity, Nazi atrocities, biographies of guilty perpetrators. In short, they did not want to know about the moral and civilizational disaster of Hitler's Germany.

The fact is that from day one in the Adenauer Republic, the signs pointed to an amnesty and the integration of the perpetrators. Creating impunity for certain State measures taken by the Nazi dictatorship was now the mainstay of the legal system – that was the point. In this way, killings and violent crimes turned into crimes ordered "from above", with no personal responsibility applied. The perpetrators and their actions were whitewashed, having allegedly not committed their own crimes, but, to a certain extent, a "foreign" act. In a way, they carried out their duties vicariously on behalf of the Nazi Party, the people and the country, and did so bound by an oath. Where obedience was the highest virtue, the fulfillment of such could not be seen as a bad thing. It was a spirit that led worthy citizens to blindly follow reprehensible, degrading, and inhumane orders because most other people were doing the same. An order was an order.

At the end of 1949, this reinterpretation of the past began with a first impunity law, passed unanimously by the Bundestag in expeditated circumstances, and which amnestied all crimes committed before 15 September 1949, punishable by a prison sentence of up to six months. A good 80,000 people benefited from this. A special paragraph explicitly granted impunity for those who, as National Socialist officials and members of the SS, had preferred to evade denazification procedures by providing false information about their identity after 1945.

Under pressure from the right-wing FDP, from 1950 onwards this impunity law was followed by several Bundestag debates in which the end of denazification was repeatedly demanded. Nothing else was requested here apart from "end point thinking", and with the so-called "131 law", a large amnesty was actually achieved for all those who could be reinstated and cared for as "repressed civil servants" or professional soldiers.

The German tendency to hide the fundamentally unjust character of the Nazi regime and its wars of conquest from the collective consciousness was thus implemented by the Adenauer government. The courts in particular showed little inclination to hold former Nazi perpetrators to account, especially since, as was well known, there was a particularly strong continuity of personnel with the Nazi era. The willingness to investigate and act in Nazi criminal cases was almost zero.

There were exceptions: Fritz Bauer, Attorney General in Hesse and a Social Democrat of Jewish origin, was one of the few unencumbered lawyers who held a leading position in the young German Federal Republic and hated nothing more than the common forms of defense such as apology and bewilderment. Bauer pushed through the abolition of the statute of limitations for Nazi murders, and without him the great Frankfurt Auschwitz trial of 1963 would not have taken place. Without this trial against former extermination camp guards, the German public would have "run away" from Nazi crimes for much longer. Fritz Bauer forced the Germans to look closer despite, and in the midst of, a judiciary that was still interspersed with former Party members. "When I leave my office, I enter hostile foreign countries," is how he once described his situation in a later television interview.

Bauer clearly recognized that the Nazi state was not a historical industrial accident and pointed to the structures and mentalities that had become ingrained over time, which had consequently helped to accommodate the Nazis' crimes so much and which would now require much more to break them up than simple court proceedings. In doing so, Bauer not only incurred the wrath of conservative circles, but was also shunned, battled and threatened. In a post-war justice system that had restored continuity with that seen under the Nazis, he was regarded as a heretic, even if many others felt the same way as he did.

An example is the Jewish journalist Inge Deutschkron, who had survived the Nazi terror by hiding in Berlin. When she came to Bonn in 1955, she was more than angry, not just because it was a provincial town that was difficult for a Berliner to bear, but above all because former Nazis were once again sitting in various high positions of power and were now unashamedly announcing that they wanted to build democracy. "I found that a bit strange. . . "

At that time there was also a man acting as State Secretary in the Chancellery, in the provincial federal capital of Bonn, whom no one in the Adenauer Republic could ignore: Dr Hans Josef Maria Globke. An exemplary criminal figure and a prototype of the smooth operator. As a lawyer and ministerial official in the Nazi Reich Ministry of the Interior, he had co-authored the first legal commentary on the "Nuremberg Race Laws" in 1936, providing detailed explanations of their practical application, enriched with case studies, which would serve the "purity of German blood".

Marriages and extramarital sexual intercourse between Jews and non-Jews were punished as "racial defilement". The comments made by the desk-jockey criminal Globke were not just words on paper, but instead provided the legal legitimacy for harsh punishments, so that as a result, people were even sentenced to death for "acts similar to coitus".

In any case, Globke's employer, Reich Minister of the Interior Wilhelm Frick, was very satisfied with his man, who, as a former member of the Catholic Center Party, was not a member of the

NSDAP but was now a zealous civil servant loyal to his National Socialist duties. On 25 April 1938, Frick wrote in a proposal for his promotion: "Senior Government Minister Globke is undoubtedly one of the most efficient and capable officials in my ministry." Globke remained in his post until the fall of the Third Reich, even after Heinrich Himmler had replaced Frick as Minister of the Interior. An ever dutiful official, he was a loyal servant of the State to the bitter end.

After the war, Globke suddenly appeared to lose his memory. He had proven himself with his legal work in the Nazi system and now became Adenauer's most important aide as the quiet General Secretary and Treasurer of the CDU. A man for all seasons, he was secretive, loyal, well-connected, could switch between systems, adapt, but never take responsibility for his actions or, what was worse, identify with the systems he served. Adaptability and expertise helped him to consolidate his position in every situation and to save his own skin.

Later, Alexander and Margarete Mitscherlich aptly described his role in their book *Die Unfähigkeit zu trauern* (*The Inability to Mourn*): "National Socialist rule would never have come to an end because of Globke and his ilk. For Globke, the line of identification with the racial laws of his superiors at the time would have remained; Globke would have died as one of the representatives of this National Socialist policy, having continued to serve as a representative of the Catholic Center Party had the Weimar Republic not collapsed."

The well-off pensioner died on 13 February 1973 in Bonn as a respected member of the community and a committed member of the local Rotary Club. Globke's career had been actively supported and promoted by Adenauer, for whom political pragmatism was more important than morality. His motto: "When establishing important ministries, you cannot do without the cooperation of experienced people from the outset."

Above all, the acceptance of numerous former Nazi diplomats into the Foreign Ministry of Adenauer's government is proof of this. At the beginning of the 1950s, around two-thirds of the senior civil servants and around four-fifths of the department heads were former NSDAP members. The figures were not much different in other ministries.

Hans Josef Maria Globke had a particularly successful German career: from Nazi lawyer to the grey eminence of the Bonn Republic. However, it was by no means an unusual one. Tens of thousands of lawyers, doctors, entrepreneurs, journalists, and officers, who had all held important roles in the Nazi regime, continued their careers in the German Federal Republic, equipped with *"Persilscheine"* (clean bills) and were thus successfully "denazified". Examples include Josef Abs, Hans Filbinger, Reinhard Gehlen, Werner Höfer, Erich Manstein, Josef Neckermann and many others.

The continuity of personnel after 1945 is a dubious lesson in political behavior between punishment and reintegration, control and infiltration, reform and restoration. Yet it was not only in offices and courtrooms where former participants reentered the world, they also found themselves in the federal armed forces and the police, as well as governmental departments and the secret services.

It is a shameful fact that the perpetrators of the Third Reich were not marginalized, persecuted or even convicted. To a certain extent, the generation of perpetrators and that of their children made a cross-generational pact: a complicity that renounced consistent exclusion, prosecution and conviction. The Adenauer era made a great peace with the perpetrators. What their grandfathers and fathers had done, what they had allowed to happen and why they had looked the other way, was only later questioned in the 1960s.

Is there a collective guilt? Or is it an individual morality, or a completely personal guilt? And are not all those who suppress the past or even deny its existence complicit? The publicist Ralph Giordano coined the phrase "secondary guilt" for such a sentiment.

Who were the perpetrators of the National Socialist war of extermination? Were they animals or followers of orders, disinterested bureaucrats and weak-willed cogs in a machine? Were they ideologized men of conviction or ordinary criminals? For decades, historians have focused almost exclusively on the main perpetrators Hitler, Himmler and Heydrich, or even on desk clerks such as Eichmann, and left out those on the second and third levels, the ones on the ground who carried the orders out.

Yes-men, hangers-on, followers of orders, accomplices, perpetrators, the definitions were fluid, the smooth transition situational. "That is why, contrary to what historical folklore suggests, even a totalitarian system such as National Socialism could rely on the flexibility of humankind, not on the rigid, inflexible mode of function," state the authors Michael Pauen and Harald Welzer, who have paid particular study to perpetrator biographies for years and question the underlying patterns, influences, experiences and decisions of those involved.

Various studies have illustrated how one might become a perpetrator, a criminal who follows orders, and how extreme the willingness to follow orders can be. These are not sadistic enforcers, but "ordinary men", who become mass murderers when peer pressure and the situation require it – or should one say, enable it?

One case that vividly illustrates the tension between refusal and participation concerns the incidents surrounding the Reserve Police Battalion 101, about which Christopher Browning has reported on in detail and which Pauen and Welzer cite as an example of the pressure to conform within military-police groups. "On the morning of 13 July 1943, the men of Reserve Battalion 101 lined up. The commander, 53-year-old Wilhelm Trapp, who was very popular with his men, was pale and nervous about what he had to say. . ." He told the 500 members of his troop that there were Jews in Jozefow (a town in east-central Poland) who were in league with the partisans. The battalion was now under orders to find these Jews, round them up, and then separate the men of working age so that they could be transported to a labor camp. All others (women, children and the elderly), were to be liquidated on the spot. He then made his men an extraordinary offer: those who did not feel up to the task could step aside, meaning they were in control of whether they wanted to participate in the mass murder. Stay in line, or stand down? Only ten or twelve men made use of Trapp's offer – 448 of them stayed put.

But what was it that drove them to become murderers? Loyalty, peer pressure, or fear of potential consequences? In any case, according to Pauen and Welzer, regardless of National Socialist sentiment or individual moral beliefs, what mattered most was the pressure to conform. In war, soldiers never act alone; the feeling of togetherness dominates everything else. The role of the group, unit, or battalion is more important for the behavior of the individual soldier than any ideological, political or personal motives they might otherwise have.

So, does what apply for the soldier also apply to "ordinary" Germans? Did they just go along with what was happening? Did they look away because everyone else was looking away? The purges and arrests, the expulsions and imprisonments, the Stars of David and the book burnings – almost everyone could see what was going on.

That Jews could no longer ride bicycles, use the tram, shop at any time of day they wished, keep pets or subscribe to newspapers; raids against and arrests of members of the opposition, death sentences issued by the People's Court on blood-red placards that were posted publicly – whoever wanted to see it could see it, experience it, or hear about it.

Is coming to terms with the past a lifelong lie for Germans? Is it a legal, social and political misnomer? Can what happened be overcome at all?

There is no doubt that on day zero after Hitler, there were people in this country who felt shame and sadness about what had happened in the years before. But the fact is that even then there were far more people who, having escaped the catastrophe, repressed what they had experienced and what had happened, instead of accepting it as their own history and being aware of their responsibility. They were a people on the run from their own past.

In Berlin today, the visualization of the past follows another line. The focus now is not on the denial and suppression of the Adenauer era, nor on the questions of the skeptical generation of the 1970s about the guilt and complicity of their fathers and grandfathers. On the one hand, controversial debates about the new culture of remembrance determine public discussion, such as those surrounding the Berlin Holocaust Memorial, for example. On the other hand, the memory of the crimes committed under National Socialism is subject to relativization, which is primarily about "German victims": the incendiary bombs on German cities, the crimes of Stalinism – cruel realities indeed. Of course, the sequence, causalities and dimensions of terror are often generously dispensed with in such cases.

Does the post-war generation to which I belong, that generation which, to quote former Chancellor Kohl, was blessed with the "grace of late birth", finally want to draw a line under a burdened history that is not too far in the past? Has this politically and morally blameless generation finally been released from the confrontation with the Hitler regime and its legacy? Or, does the responsibility of this generation begin with the question of how they feel about the guilt of their grandparents and parents? Does it want to remember?

This book focusses on four perpetrators:

The military lawyer **Erich Schwinge**, who, after his dubious Nazi work at the University of Marburg, made an academic career as a law professor, commentator and author and became a respected citizen of the city.

Arnold Strippel, who left a trail of blood as a brutal concentration camp guard in numerous camps. He was initially imprisoned after the war but was then acquitted on appeal and released soon afterwards, before receiving a large sum of money as compensation for loss of earnings. As a pensioner, he lived a quiet life, appreciated by his neighbors, in a tranquil village near Frankfurt am Main.

Roland Freisler was the President of the People's Court who sentenced the Scholl siblings, the resistance fighters of 20 July and more than 3,000 other "enemies of the state and defeatists" to death. As the widow of a senior Nazi state official, his wife, Marion Russegger, was well taken care of by the Bavarian state and benefited from the regular increases in the pension fund until her death.

Finally, the executioner **Johann Reichhart**, who worked for three different employers: the Weimar Republic, National Socialism and later in Landsberg under the American occupation forces. Between 1924 and 1945 he carried out 3,126 executions – 250 of whom were women. Those killed included murderers and violent criminals, but also resistance fighters and alleged opponents of the Nazi regime. He then hanged a further 156 people on the orders of the American military powers.

A special, although not infrequently stated, ambivalence can be found in his biography in particular: the proximity of the perpetrator's arbitrariness to the fate of the victim in one person. Johann Reichhart was a vicarious agent, the receiver of orders and executor of them, who in the end, found himself accused and an outcast. Stripped of his civil rights after being put on trial, he died shortly before his 79th birthday in a Bavarian hospital, near Munich, in 1974.

Anyone who writes about perpetrators always writes about victims as well. In the concluding chapter, two men are featured who did not know each other, but who paid for the same act with their lives. **Georg Elser** and **Maurice Bavaud** were two Hitler assassins who, without any support from other conspirators, dared to do "it" earlier than anyone else. Both were murdered by the National Socialists. Arrest, trial and murder – the Germans allowed it with indifferent consent. After the war, their names were erased, like most of the victims of Hitler's dictatorship, and it took over sixty years for their fate to be recognized.

One final thing: I spoke to many eyewitnesses during the research for these dossiers. Those who stood before the People's Court and were sentenced to death, only to survive solely because the end of the war preceded their execution. People who, as judges, applied Nazi laws and passed merciless sentences, often with fatal consequences for those convicted. Some of these people – it is my impression – were still able to live perfectly well with this heavy weight on their shoulders. They felt that they had been "innocently burdened" and that their faith in the Fatherland had been abused by "politicians". Hardly any of them acknowledged their personal responsibility and showed little trace of remorse or shame. On the contrary, they often even regarded themselves as being victims of a "fateful time".

Some of them still live among us. In old age, well provided for with equally high pensions from the state treasury. Most still believe that they were simply doing their duty at the time. They were simply normal people, who today live as part of our normal society.

The perpetrators are dying out – as are the victims and eyewitnesses. With a view to the present, in which personal remembrance is becoming increasingly rare, it is important to know how "it could have happened", and not just the willingness to remember. The references and bibliography at the end of the book may help.

Above all, Detmold's guilty verdict against the aged former SS man Hanning remains a symbol that reminds us of what happened – and must never happen again.

THE "HONORABLE" GENTLEMAN FROM MARBURG
HOW A MILITARY JUDGE MADE A CAREER AFTER 1945

On a sultry summer day in August 1984, an old, well-dressed gentleman with rimless glasses entered the *Dokumentationsarchiv des österreichischen Widerstandes* (Document Center of Austrian Resistance) on Vienna's Wipplingerstraße. He introduced himself as the Emeritus law professor Erich Schwinge from Marburg, in the Federal Republic of Germany, and requested access to the file on "Anton Reschny". He was led into the reading room, where he studied and took notes on all kinds of documents for the next two to three hours.

On 23 August 1944, just a week after becoming a soldier and having not yet received his orders, a Viennese vulcanization apprentice called Anton Reschny had volunteered to help clean up after a bombing raid and stole a ring, two watches, a purse and an empty wallet from a prosecutor's apartment. The 17-year-old gave one of the watches to a girl, who proudly showed it around. Six days later, Reschny was arrested.

On 14 September 1944, Divisional Court 177, presided over by the military judge Erich Schwinge, sentenced the young Anton Reschny to death for looting. Schwinge's explanation for his judgment: "The accused. . .claims to have been unaware of the magnitude of his actions. In determining the sentence, the death penalty has to be imposed, assuming it is a particularly serious case within the meaning of paragraph 2, section 129, of the Military Criminal Code." The defendant had "in the field [i.e. in the war] taken advantage of the war situation by taking items that belonged to the German people. . .with the intention of unlawfully appropriating them." What is more: "Criminal elements who have an innate desire to enrich themselves with the property of bomb victims must know that they are risking their heads if they indulge this inclination; otherwise, such elements cannot be kept in check."

There was a reason why Schwinge, almost forty years to the month after he sentenced the apprentice to death, had sought out his own story in the Vienna archive.

What obviously drove him on such a research spree were publications about his work during the Nazi era as a leading commentator on military criminal law and, above all, as a military judge in Vienna. The private researcher Fritz Wüllner, a retired business manager, had discovered numerous papers and documents when trying to learn the fate of his brother, who was allegedly shot "while trying to escape", and in the process came across a bad chapter of Nazi history that until then had received little attention: military justice.

Wüllner, who had researched domestic and foreign archives, had found next to nothing about his brother. However, he was enraged to discover numerous inconsistencies in the historiography of Nazi military justice: "So I became interested in military justice. . . Whoever I asked about my inquiries, again and again I was referred to the standard work by Schweling and Schwinge, *Die deutsche Militärjustiz in der Zeit des Nationalsozialismus* [*German Military Justice in the Time of National Socialism*], published in 1977. I bought it, read it, and was horrified!"

Wüllner continues: "Even a layman should have immediately realized that this writing was not just an apology, but misleading and deceptive from the very beginning. Yes, I would go even further, in some ways it is fraud. . . "

From then on, refuting Schwinge's book provided the driving force behind Fritz Wüllner's search for clues. Erich Schwinge – professor emeritus and military judge – had already emerged as a particularly harsh commentator on the Nazi military penal code as early as 1936, and therefore considered himself capable of publishing the post-war book on German military justice – a work from which his initial client, the renowned Institute of Contemporary History in Munich, later distanced itself.

The original author of the work was Otto Peter Schweling, Senior Public Prosecutor at the Federal Prosecutor's Office, who was also a former military judge. After his death, Schwinge acquired the rights and acted as editor of the controversial work, which some reviewers called a "hymn of praise" to military justice and "clearly partisan". Fritz Wüllner also quickly recognized the various contradictions in Schwinge's book. His initial impressions were further justified after visiting the Federal Archives in Koblenz. After intensive research, he was only able to find one sentence to say that during the war there were around 700,000 trials presented before German military courts: "That is not even half the truth." The cruel balance sheet shows that a total of around 2.5 million criminal proceedings were dealt with by the German military judiciary, with more than 30,000 of these cases being sentenced to death.

But it was not only in Koblenz that Wüllner found what he was looking for. By chance, he learned that military justice files are stored not only in Potsdam, but also in Vienna. His research into the dusty accounts of a repressed past repeatedly led him to the mountains of files for Divisional Court 177, where Schwinge passed judgements or brought charges from 1941 until the bitter end. Between January 1944 and February 1945 alone, seven death sentences were signed. As a prosecutor, Schwinge applied for a further nine more during this period, including one on 9 February 1945. In his desperation, the defendant had injected himself with petroleum in the hope it would prevent him from being deployed to the front. As a result of "undermining military authority", the young soldier was put on trial. When giving reasons for his verdict, Schwinge writes: "In a highly critical situation, the defendant avoided going to the front, and in doing so set a very dangerous example for his comrades. In the interests of discipline, such a breach of duty can only be countered by the severest punishment – the death penalty."

However, Schwinge was not solely responsible for the merciless judgments he demanded and made. Yet as a well-known commentator and the only colleague with a professorship, he had great influence. A man of his rank could naturally influence proceedings not only as a prominent judge or prosecutor, but also as an investigative judge and researcher. This he did, but of course only in the sense of Nazi Wehrmacht justice. In the last phase of the war – as with everywhere in the dying Reich – the number of death sentences pronounced by the Divisional Court 177 increased to a frightening degree. Even when the Russians were already lining up before the city, decisions between life and death were still being made. For the most part, the military lawyers in their Nazi uniforms proclaimed the death penalty. Schwinge was one of the more fanatical Nazi war judges. "An unusually zealous and hard-working judge with very good knowledge, good negotiation skills and a sure judgement. . ." So said the official assessment of Schwinge, who, in addition to his work as a judge, also taught young students as a professor at the University of Vienna.

Numerous essays from this period testify that this was an extremely strict representation of National Socialist ideas. *Die Behandlung der Psychopathen im Militärstrafrecht* (*The Treatment of Psychopaths in Military Criminal Law*) (1939/40) speaks of "negative types", "inferiors" and their "intensive disruptive work". Ernst Toller, a member of the Munich council government in 1919, who had volunteered for the First World War but became a pacifist at the front, is described as a "baseless, abnormal person", and an "ethically defective and fanatical psychopath". Schwinge describes the pacifist writer and socialist politician Erich Mühsam, who was murdered by the Nazis at Oranienburg concentration camp in 1934, as an "even more dangerous type of psychopath".

In Schwinge's words: "Nothing can do better than these two names to illustrate what damage such inferior people can do in times of national distress if society is not protected from them!"

According to Schwinge, there was no place in the world of National Socialism for "inferiors", "weaklings" or "failures". Military lawyers in particular see young men unable to cope psychologically with the barrage of a murderous war as slackers who must not be shown the slightest benefit of the doubt. No, they should not be sent to serve on the Home Front, Schwinge argued. Instead, they should be grouped together in special "psychopath companies".

The "disruptive" point of view is particularly pertinent to him because it is crucial that "the elements withdrawn from the troop as a whole are thereby rendered incapable of poisoning the minds of their comrades". To completely release those concerned from the discipline of the Wehrmacht – which sometimes happened with neurotics during the First World War by order of the War Ministry – would not be advisable. "If they feel relieved of their military duties, they will immediately resume their disruptive work at home and continue it with increased vigor. Thus, the enrichment of the homeland with such inferior elements carries hardly less dangers than their use in combat troops. Finally, the demoralizing effect of these bad examples must also be taken into account."

Dismissal would act as a sort of bonus, which would drive the abnormal to the worst excesses. "In contrast, in a future war, a great deal of work must be done right from the start. The psychopaths assigned to special units must remain close to the front and be engaged in work that exposes them to as much danger as their fellow comrades in the troop. A one-sided 'counter-selection' war against the good and valuable elements of our society must not happen again. It is unacceptable for the best to lay down their lives at the front while the physically and mentally inferior cause unrest in the homeland."

There is no question that lines like these prove Schwinge was a merciless judge. As early as 1933 he was a cell leader in the *Bund Nationalsozialistischer Deutscher Juristen* (League of National Socialist German Lawyers) and frequently volunteered in military exercises after 1935. He was the kind of judge the Nazis needed. After the end of the war, his eagerness to serve was by no means his undoing. On the contrary, like so many ex-Nazi judges, he had a successful career, becoming a law professor at the University of Marburg, dean, and even rector. In a commemorative publication entitled *Persönlichkeit in der Demokratie* (*Personality in Democracy*), published by colleagues in 1973 on the occasion of Schwinge's 70th birthday, there is nothing but praise for him.

His numerous publications, it is said, "have carried the author's teachings of the freedom of man, the preservation of his dignity, freedom of thought and the paramount importance of legal process into wider circles". Examples include his legal writings such as *Bilanz der Kriegsgeneration* (*Balance Sheet of the War Generation*), which was first published in 1979 and then saw a further ten editions, or his book *Verfälschung und Wahrheit*, (*Falsification and Truth*), which came out in 1988 and in which he portrays Hitler's military judiciary almost as an opponent of National Socialism.

In its brochure, the Hohenrain publishing house in Tübingen calls its author Schwinge the "last surviving German expert on military criminal law" and one of the "most successful contemporary German lawyers". The reader also learns that one of Schwinge's books was banned in 1940. Could he possibly be seen as a resistance fighter? A secret opponent dressed in Nazi robes? In the foreword to his 1983 book *Der Staatsmann – Anspruch und Wirklichkeit* (*Statesman – Pretense and Reality*), the military lawyer almost comes across as an upstanding humanist: "It is high time that a period of reflection is called for here. This is necessary because the frightening decline in statecraft that has occurred in our century must be stopped. This decline is particularly evident in the way in which human lives are dealt with today. The first great turn to inhumanity that killed millions of people was not carried out by Lenin and then continued – on a gigantic scale – by Stalin and Hitler, rather it began even before then, in the camp of Western democracies."

What about Schwinge and human life? Had he forgotten – or did this "terrible lawyer" (Rolf Hochhuth) want to make people forget – how he himself dealt with human lives during the Nazi era and how the German military justice system, which he had a major influence on, dealt with them? Thanks to the persistent and comprehensive investigations by the private researcher Fritz Wüllner, the gaps in Schwinge's memory can be filled in with truths.

In Wüllner's 1991 book *Die NS-Militärjustiz und das Elend der Geschichtsschreibung* (*Nazi Military Justice and the Misery of Historiography*), excerpts of ten death sentences issued by the Divisional Court 177 in Vienna are documented. Until his capture in May 1945, Schwinge helped to send people to their deaths as a judge, prosecutor and lawyer. Frightening verdicts are discussed in detail in Wüllner's research work, all from the last phase of the war. At that time, when the "Thousand Year Reich" was sinking into ruins, hundreds of thousands of people were already on the run, and the end of the war was imminent, Schwinge and his colleagues were still handing down death sentences for desertion, degradation of military force, and recidivism. "Deterrence" as a justification for the death sentence had long since become a farce, but Schwinge and his cronies mercilessly passed sentence until the end. Here are two perfect examples:

Gunner Heinz Sorbe, born 22 June 1918 in Frankfurt am Main, was sentenced to death on 15 February 1944 by Divisional Court

177, presided over by Schwinge, for desertion and repeated theft (*Str. L. No. II/1193/1943*). The gunner's war record is summarized in Wüllner's report:

Sorbe had volunteered for the Reich Labor Service in mid-1935 and, after completing his labor service, volunteered for the Wehrmacht, which he joined on 7 March 1940. After taking part in the French campaign, he was arrested in August 1940 and was sentenced by the court of Div. No. 159 in Frankfurt to the outrageous punishment of three years in prison for unauthorized removal. On 9 November 1942 he was sentenced again in Vienna, this time for bicycle theft, to one year in prison, an equally excessive sentence and presumably due to his previous conviction. [At that time, bicycle thefts took place almost non-stop in all major cities. Soldiers who stole bicycles usually left them elsewhere on the same day or a few days later.] After he began his sentence in January 1943, it was ordered that further punishment should take place in a combat prisoner detachment, starting in March 1943. Following a foot wound sustained in Russia during this deployment to a combat prisoner detachment, he was admitted to a military hospital at the main dressing station in Voroshilovsk. On 13 July 1943 he took advantage of an opportunity to leave the field hospital and made his way through Russia to Upper Silesia. In the following years he stayed in Vienna, then Kitzingen, where he learned that his mother had died, before returning to Frankfurt and then finally back to Vienna. He was arrested on 7 November 1943 but was able to flee again on 24 November. Shortly thereafter, he was arrested again.

The verdict was confirmed on 9 March 1944, and the young man would have been unwise to count on any mercy. His request for clemency was rejected, and the sentence was carried out on 24 May 1944. The executioner (Reichhart) and three assistants beheaded Heinz Sorbe at 19:12. It was perfectly in the spirit of Schwinge, who in the last sentence of the verdict had stated: "Such a dereliction of duty can only be atoned for in the interests of public safety and military discipline by the sacrifice of one's life."

Another example is Grenadier Bela Tesch, born in Oedenburg on 20 August 1904, who was sentenced to death by Divisional Court 177 on 13 January 1945 for desertion (Str. L. No. H/1252/44). The death sentence was once again requested by the representative of the prosecution, Chief Staff Judge Dr Schwinge. Wüllner documents what Schwinge's had to say:

> *The defendant had been drafted into the Wehrmacht on 1 July 1943. On 14 August 1943, after six weeks of training with the troops, he used a night leave to leave Vienna, cross the German border unnoticed and return to his family in Oedenburg. He stayed in Oedenburg until 19 March 1944. When the German troops marched into Hungary at this time, he disappeared from Oedenburg and was only arrested on 11 October 1944 by a German Wehrmacht patrol near Oedenburg.*

In the last paragraph of the judgment, Schwinge again shows himself to be the master of life and death:

> *The defendant committed the desertion abroad and in doing so committed a serious crime against the German Reich. He was active as an anti-German agitator, who listened to enemy radio stations and urged his comrades to commit similar crimes. He was able to remain absent without leave for over a year. The fact he was also active as a communist leader could not be established in this context. The defendant, however, engaged in criminal activities to a considerable extent during his desertion.*
>
> *In the sixth year of the war, at a time when all elements of the German people are fighting in the final struggle for existence, in order to maintain discipline and to act as a deterrent, the only necessary and just punishment for this desertion is the death penalty.*

On 3 April 1945, just a few days before Russian troops took Vienna, the young Bela Tesch was shot after a request for clemency had been rejected. A transcript states soberly: "The execution squad of six men was positioned five paces in front of the condemned man. The command to fire took place at 18:49. The prisoner died calmly and like a soldier."

Justifications for judgments such as these did not harm Schwinge in post-war Germany. As early as 1946 he was teaching law and was also a regular contributor to the *Neue Zeitschrift für Wehrrecht* (*New Journal for Military Law*), for which he had already written articles during the Nazi era, when it was still called the *Zeitschrift für Wehrrecht*. At this time, a word like "new" was enough for a "new career", and Schwinge pursued one as a scientist, professor and publicist at breakneck speed.

Like many perpetrators, he was on the winners' side. In the early 1950s, a man with his past could even make it to deputy FDP chairman of Hesse, and in his hometown of Marburg an der Lahn, he was one of the city's celebrities. Until the mid-1980s, Professor Dr Schwinge lived a quiet, well-to-do life of retirement and wrote numerous books in which he discussed his proven interpretation of history and practiced whitewashing and coming to terms with the past. He was not without success, always finding grateful readers in Germany, and would have remained an honored and respected man, had it not been for Fritz Wüllner, who researched the covert structures of military justice in the Nazi era and Schwinge's career like no other before. In the records of the State Archives in Vienna, Fritz Wüllner found the files of the death sentence pronounced against Anton Reschny by Schwinge in 1944. A young man sent to the scaffold just because he stole a few small items?

The Reschny case is an unusual story. Why? Because unlike the two young soldiers, Sorge and Tesch, Reschny survived his death sentence. In spite of Schwinge. At the time, the apprentice was accused, quite correctly, of violating the so-called *Volksschädlingsverordnung* (public nuisance order). The Juvenile Court Act, which did not allow such draconian punishments, would have been applicable in this case. Instead, Schwinge resorted to the military penal code, which excluded protection from the death penalty for juveniles. For simple cases of looting, "prison or imprisonment in a fortress" was given as punishment, with imprisonment or the death penalty only given in "particularly serious cases". Schwinge, however, justified his verdict on Reschny by saying that "every case of looting" in big cities "must lead to the death penalty without exception". After all, criminals should know "that they are risking their heads". Ironically, it was Heinrich Himmler who pardoned Anton

Reschny. In this case, the notorious SS leader was more insightful than the fanatical Nazi judge and commuted the sentence to fifteen years in prison.

Fritz Wüllner went to Austria and visited Reschny, who was living as a pensioner in Vienna. After detailed discussions with him, he returned with a power of attorney and used it to commission the Frankfurt lawyer Stefan Baier to file a criminal complaint against Schwinge "for attempted murder".

Others who had heard about the "Reschny case" had already done this, including the Austrian resistance fighter Eduard Rabofsky in Vienna, and the Hildesheim judge Ulrich Vultejus at the law enforcement authorities in Marburg. Now another was added. According to this third criminal complaint "for attempted murder and perversion of justice", Schwinge had tried "to kill the 17-year-old by legal means" by illegally using military criminal law instead of the public nuisance law, in what he had decreed to be a "particularly serious" case of looting. As a law professor and one of the leading commentators on the military penal code, according to the lawyer Baier, Schwinge knew very well that, based on the applicable law, he should have sentenced "Reschny to a maximum of ten years in prison". The Frankfurt lawyer relied on the case law of the Federal Court of Justice, according to which, a criminal judge perverts the course of justice "if he deliberately imposes a penalty which, in terms of type or amount, is unbearably disproportionate to the seriousness of the crime and the guilt of the perpetrator". The fact that, as Baier notes, it was "the first thoughtless act of a 17-year-old", that no "violence or special cunning" was used and "that the value of the items was not very high" had all been ignored by Schwinge.

However, Marburg's chief prosecutor, Kohl, did not want to agree with the lawyer's well-substantiated allegations. According to the lawyer, the application of military criminal law was justifiable because the "vague and wide-ranging" elements of the facts would have been "broadly interpreted" at the time. The public prosecutor considered the imposition of the death

11

penalty to be inappropriate because the Nazi judge would not have taken into account any mitigating factors. However, the Marburg public prosecutor's opinion was not enough to uphold the charge of attempted murder and perversion of justice. It was "absolutely not unjustifiable," Kohl noted in his ruling, that Schwinge had assumed Rechny to have committed a particularly serious case of looting, because "in times of war and distress, strict standards in the application of criminal law tend to develop everywhere". Thanks to this, Erich Schwinge, who in several statements for the Marburg public prosecutor's office had tried to explain in detail why he wanted to achieve deterrence with the death sentence, legally restructured his old-world view. Yet Baier and Reschny, as well as the industrious Wüllner, were not satisfied with the decision. Baier not only considered the legal considerations of the Marburg public prosecutor to be inadmissible and unfounded, but also discovered all sorts of gaps and omissions in the investigation into the case. First of all was Schwinge's claim that he had advocated a pardon for Reschny immediately after the verdict. It is undisputed that the war code of criminal procedure at the time stipulated judges of a court martial had to comment in writing on the question of pardon after a death sentence had been pronounced. Schwinge stated that he voted for it, yet Fritz Wüllner found no "pardon papers" written by Schwinge in the Vienna archives, despite an intensive search of the files.

This means there is no reliable proof that Schwinge advocated clemency for Reschny at the time. Besides, what made Schwinge so confident in the assumption that Himmler, of all people, would overturn the death sentence against Reschny? Schwinge had repeatedly highlighted the necessarily deterrent nature of having to point out "Those elements that were on the move", which in Reschny's case meant looting. Hence the harsh verdict. But there is hardly any compelling logic to this argument, especially when one knows that the verdict, which was intended to serve as a deterrent, was not announced in the young soldier's former unit or elsewhere – only the condemned man's parents knew about it. So much for a general deterrence.

There were a lot of unanswered questions about the legal situation and the facts, and the matter should have been dealt with by the Hessian Attorney General, as Baier had wanted. But even there, the complaint against Schwinge remained unsuccessful because the statute of limitations had expired and there was no intent to kill, meaning charges against Schwinge were dropped. The notification Baier received stated: "According to the will of the Nazi rulers, members of the Wehrmacht should be held strictly and unforgivingly, but at least legally, responsible for crimes they have committed."

In the case of Anton Reschny, who was sentenced to death, the statute of limitations for prosecution had expired in August 1965. Thus, only the enforcement of the lawsuit remained, and this was also ultimately rejected with the remarkable comment that the allegations made by Reschny were "unfounded"! For his part, Schwinge presented the Marburg Chief Public Prosecutor with an affidavit from his former division commander, Erich Müller Derichweiler. In this statement from 9 September 1946, the general seems to admit that he deliberately assigned "difficult cases" to Erich Schwinge at the time, "because I knew he would use all his knowledge and ability to protect the defendants from the merciless harshness of National Socialist legislation". He therefore considered Schwinge to be particularly suitable "as an educator and teacher of young people".

In Marburg an der Lahn, high above the city in his whitewashed villa in the dignified residential district of Orteberg, Professor Dr Erich Schwinge looked down on "his" university. As an emeritus professor and former rector, he was still listed in the personnel directory of Philipps University and still enjoyed the privilege of having a study reserved especially for him. Whether at his desk at home or in his professor's office, he still kept himself busy. He wrote essays, gave lectures, and published books, continuing to provide for the patriotic die-hards and the unteachables of today, including his 1991 book *Bundeswehr und Wehrmacht – Zum Problem der Traditionswürdigkeit* (*Bundeswehr and Wehrmacht – On the Problem of Tradition*), in which he refers to the great achievements of the "German soldier" and calls for its "restoration of honor". Under the chapter heading "The military performance of the Wehrmacht and its soldiers", Schwinge, in his tried and tested judge's tone, takes issue with all opponents of the Wehrmacht. According to him, the image left behind by the German soldier and the German Wehrmacht in the occupied eastern territories was enough to "to refute the claims of one-sided historians with their judgement of condemnation". His view of Hitler's army was that: "Seen as a whole, it is honorable and, because of its exemplary character, suitable to be recognized and treated as worthy of tradition." Even the "leading military officers on the Allied side" were united in their judgement. Schwinge had been right: "The German soldiers they had encountered could only be described as first-class."

On the final page, the military lawyer reveals to his loyal readers how to effectively counteract the character assassination campaign being pursued from all sides against German soldiers. He stated: "The next step is to restore the honor of the soldiers who once belonged to the Wehrmacht. They must be freed from the stigma of belonging to a criminal organization that covered the whole of Europe with barbaric warfare, was responsible for millions of murders, and participated in Nazi atrocities on a large scale." The preface for Schwinge's patriotic legitimation pamphlet was provided by the military practitioner, Major General Dr Jürgen Schreiber, President of the "Ring of German Soldiers' Associations" and author of justification publications with titles such as *Waren wir Täter? – Gegen die Volksverdummung unserer Zeit* (*Were We Perpetrators? – Against the Stupidity of the People of our Time*), which appeared in the August 1991 issue of the magazine *Soldat im Volk* (whose subtitle was "for the tradition and progress of European soldiering"). The preface is advertised with the following text: "This volume is the confession of a man who does not want to bow to the zeitgeist and anti-German atrocity propaganda. It is equally important for the war generation and for young people to make up their own minds." As early as 1987, in his multi-page justification collection *Bilanz der Kriegsgeneration* – to a certain extent his magnum opus – Schwinge was supported by another high-ranking general, Heinz Karst, who provided the foreword.

As an ordnance officer of the 10th Infantry Division, he had received the Iron Cross 1st Class in Russia and had later commanded an armoured reconnaissance detachment on the Eastern Front. After the war, his career progressed seamlessly. As one of the first soldiers of the Bundeswehr, Karst was given the rank of major and went to the School of Internal Leadership in Koblenz, where he then rose to head the department for education in the Federal Ministry of Defense.

Karst was regarded as an exponent of what was then still a strong traditionalist group in the upper echelons of the Bundeswehr, which was strictly opposed to the model of "inner leadership" ("citizens in uniform"). Instead of democratization, it relied on traditional concepts of command, obedience and education and forbade any criticism of the Wehrmacht. In 1964, Karst expressed his ideas about the soldier's profession in a booklet, *Das Bild des Soldaten* (*The Image of the Soldier*).

The highlight of his career was being appointed to the rank of brigadier general, where he was employed – he of all people – to educate and train the army. An ex-Wehrmacht officer, decorated with the Iron Cross and still of very strong opinions, was now responsible for the "education" of young soldiers in the Federal Republic. There is no question that the Bonn Republic also stood for continuity in the Bundeswehr.

There was also recognition for his exemplary German way of life: Heinz Karst was awarded the Grand Cross of Merit of the Federal Republic of Germany. From 1973 to 1977 he was chairman of the conservative Germany Foundation, and was also one of the founding members of the initiatives of the Hans

Filbinger Foundation – named after the CDU politician Filbinger, also a former military judge, who passed death sentences on young deserters in the last few years of the war that later forced him to resign as Prime Minister of the state of Baden-Württemberg – which was to promote a new study center in Weikersheim. In short, he was the perfect, opinionated author to write the foreword for Schwinge.

Schwinge's *Bilanz der Kriegsgeneration* went through several editions, and its content is aptly characterized in a reader's review:

> *At the language level of a mediocre professor, but at the narrative and argumentation level of Landser magazines, the author tries to hammer into the reader with the constant repetition that the German war generation achieved successes of globally-historical proportions but fell victim to the Allies' demands for unconditional surrender. Churchill was mainly to blame for the destruction of Germany, but so too was Roosevelt, while the German troops, with their unique will to persevere, saved Western Europe from a Bolshevik flood. Hitler, the genocidal SS and the Wehrmacht waging a war of aggression are not even marginal figures in this hodgepodge. And of course, the author does not speak of the disproportionate death sentences that he himself handed down as a military judge and for which, after the German judiciary had freed itself from the judicial practice of the old champions in the 1990s, should have expected an indictment and conviction for perverting the law in conjunction with capital crimes. The book is only worthwhile for those who want to find out how whitewashing and denial was carried out for half a century after 1945. Schwinge is one of very, very many . . .*

Schwinge did not want to bow to the zeitgeist either. A discussion about whether Wehrmacht deserters were "traitors to the Fatherland" or "cowards", and above all whether a monument should be erected to these men, must seem to come across as an act of anti-state sedition to him, who had always defended the process of "soldierly discipline" – if necessary, with the death sentence. In the summer of 1988, certain members of the Green Party in Marburg proposed erecting a monument to pacifists and deserters, thus triggering a heated debate in the provincial town. However, the debate only turned into a genuine issue when the commander of the Marburg garrison, Lieutenant Colonel Leyherr, commented on the matter. A monument to such lawbreakers, according to the commander of over 3,000 Bundeswehr soldiers, would be a "disgrace and an attack on the constitutional state". The commander appealed to Marburg's city fathers not to "allow themselves to be degraded" and agree to such a request. He could rest assured that with the majority of votes from the CDU and SPD groups, the parliament rejected the demand for a monument.

The provincial world of Marburg was once again in order, while Schwinge would be relieved to learn that the government in his hometown could still be relied upon. Not only with regard to Germany's value of tradition, but also in its refusal to be taught about its past. At no point had Schwinge ever indicated that, at least in retrospect, the work he carried out at the time gave him pause for thought. Anyone who tried to shed light on his own murky past had to reckon with a "decisive resistance".

For example, he complained to the German Press Council about the coverage of the *Frankfurter Rundschau*, which had reported on his time in Vienna and his post-war career. "Anyone who attacks me can count on my decisive resistance" – he had been testing this out for years. In 1964 he sued the *Illustrierte Revue* for damages of 30,000 marks – and won. Against the *Westdeutscher Rundfunk* he came to a tolerable and profitable settlement: 10,000 marks and declaration of honor. He also sued judge Ulrich Vultejus, who in his book *Kampfanzug unter der Robe* had attacked the Nazi Wehrmacht judiciary and, among other things, Schwinge. Whether journalist or student, there were "opponents" lurking everywhere who need to be fought. For example, the Marburg student Michael Lemling, who, during a panel discussion at the Marburg church convention in June 1990, discussed the topic of "Nazi Wehrmacht Justice and Desertion" and also brought up Schwinge's war record, pointing out the death sentences he had handed down and his subsequent post-war career.

Three witnesses were said to have heard him call Schwinge the "most disgusting Marburger" and an "impudent man". Among these witnesses was a right-wing fraternity member, who promptly informed the honorable military lawyer. Once again, Schwinge sought protection from the judiciary and filed criminal charges against the student for insulting him. Since the Marburg public prosecutor's office saw no public interest in the case, and after an attempt at conciliation with the arbitrator brought no further clarification, Schwinge's only option was to launch a private lawsuit.

Michael Lemling, a member of the Marburg history workshop, which had been researching and coming to terms with its local Nazi past for years, was surprised when Schwinge's lawyers withdrew the private lawsuit in November on the grounds that their client had "been strongly advised by his two doctors not to expose himself to the stresses of a court hearing".

Perhaps, however, the lawyers had convinced the controversial ex-military judge that such proceedings would eventually reignite the public debate about his past. And this time, Schwinge – for once – agreed. In any case, a short time later, the old gentleman was full of vigor again. With his head held high and his step brisk, he could be seen on his way to his study in the university, where, as a professor of law, he once taught entire generations of lawyers the necessary sense of German justice. As a man of the highest level of competence, with the best German attitude, he continued to be respected by his academic ex-colleagues as an "educator and teacher of young people". As a deserving citizen, he was honored in the city and greeted as a friendly neighbor in his local area. Quite the German lawyer's life.

The former military judge died a respected citizen on 30 April 1994 – the anniversary of Hitler's death.

"THERE HAS TO BE AN END AT SOME POINT"
THE NEIGHBOR: A CONCENTRATION CAMP MURDERER

The six men came in broad daylight and entered the stairwell, unnoticed. The preparations for a planned disturbance of the peace began: corridor walls were sprayed with slogans, leaflets scattered, windows smashed. Agitated residents stormed out of their apartments, resulting in fierce battles of words with the intruders. The first passers-by stopped in front of the house.

"Strippel, kinderhenker!" ("Strippel, child killer"), the small group of demonstrators chanted. The man, whose name was being repeatedly shouted louder and louder, stood motionless behind the curtains on the second floor, watching the scene. Arnold Strippel, who many neighbors knew as the quiet, elderly gentleman from Talstraße 10, had once again been overtaken by his past. A group of French Jews had traveled to Frankfurt, outraged that the man responsible for the murder of twenty Jewish children, who had previously been subjected to human experiments at the Neuengamme concentration camp, near Hamburg, was still at liberty. They had been preparing for this for a long time. Leaflets posted through mailboxes of the surrounding houses spoke of a "long trail of blood" that the

former concentration camp commander, Arnold Strippel, had left behind at Buchenwald, Ravensbrück, Majdanek and Peenemünde.

"Strippel, murderer!" the demonstrators continued to shout, even louder, as the angry neighbors began to become violent. "Mind your own business. Go home!", they taunted. Much tugging and jostling followed before the police finally appeared. After heated discussions and mutual accusations, the demonstrators were arrested, taken away, and brought before the magistrate. They had achieved their goal, despite the arrest, as the next day every daily newspaper in Frankfurt reported on the action against the former SS man.

And after that? The public prosecutor's office issued charges for trespassing, after not only Strippel but also his neighbors filed criminal charges against the Jewish demonstrators. A few days later, the demolished windows were replaced and the slogans – along with the memory of his uncomfortable past – were wiped from the corridor walls.

The village of Kalbach has been incorporated into the metropolis of Frankfurt for years and is now wedged in place by expressways and autobahns on the northeastern periphery of the city. The old village center consists of a few small streets, half a dozen farms and half-timbered facades; the village idyll having long since given way to urban practicality. At the entrance to the village, where a few years ago huge fields still opened up the view to the nearby Taunus mountain range, there is now a leisure center: a combination of steel, metal and colorful giant pipes. The gigantic complex seems a little oversized; a size or two too big. This formerly tranquil place wants to appear modern.

The valley road runs through the old village center, where I meet the postman: "Strippel?"

He scratches his head, almost embarrassed, "That's a delicate subject."

"Why?" I ask.

"There was something about him on television," he says hesitantly. "A trial. He was accused. Said to have done bad things. But it's difficult to prove it after such a long time. It's clear he was a concentration camp guard."

"Is this a problem for the neighbors?"

"No, that's not an issue here. . .Aggression or anything like that against him. . .No, it doesn't exist here."

I ask him when he last saw and spoke to Strippel.

"Only two weeks ago. I saw him at the door. He doesn't speak much. He's become very withdrawn since the incident a few years ago. He hardly ever leaves his apartment. His wife does the shopping. From time to time he lets his son drive him over to the spa in Bad Homburg. But otherwise, he won't leave the house."

According to the postman, Strippel had a camera installed at the window and a security lock put on the apartment door after the incident. "But afraid?" says the man with a smile, "The man doesn't need to be afraid here. Nobody is going to hurt him." The fact that Strippel is regarded by his Kalbach neighbors as a thoroughly honorable man is evidenced later when I ask an older man for his address. "What do you want from him?" he bursts out harshly, "Can't you just leave the man in peace?"

Who is this man who hardly anyone here wants to talk about, whose past no one seems to be outraged about and who no one is ashamed to have as their neighbor?

"I, Arnold Strippel, was born as the second son of the farmer Friedrich Strippel and his wife Martha, *née* Wald, on 4 June 1911 in Unshausen, in the district of Kassel," he wrote in his CV for the *"Rasse und Siedlungshauptamt SS"* (SS Race and Settlement Office). "From the age of 6 to 14 I attended elementary school there. After leaving school, I learned carpentry in my uncle's workshop. Even after passing the journeyman's examination, which I took after a three-year apprenticeship, I stayed with my teacher and, later, when the construction business collapsed, worked at my parents' farm. In spring 1934, I applied for a position in the SS."

21

Arnold Strippel was accepted, meeting the requirements both outwardly and inwardly; a blond Germanic warrior 1.85 metres tall, who, according to the reports filed by the SS doctors, was both "upstanding" and "Nordic".

In October 1934, Arnold Strippel began his service with the SS guards at Sachsenberg concentration camp. It was the beginning of a bloody SS career, and there would be few concentration camps he would not see in the next few years. Just four years later, he was a *Rapportführer* at Buchenwald concentration camp, where one of his tasks was to punish the detainees.

"Corporal punishment was carried out on the trestle table, on which the prisoner in question was laid, with his back strapped tight," the Frankfurt jury later heard in 1949. "The punishment was five to twenty-five lashes. In the early days, a cane the width of a finger was used, but from the end of 1938 onwards, short leather whips and finally bull whips were used instead."

Strippel was feared by the camp inmates, who considered him to be particularly brutal, an evil thug and a tormentor. Later, a witness in court would say about him: "Strippel was a man who attached the greatest importance to carrying out his duties 100 percent. I saw him repeatedly beat people with pleasure. . . He kicked old people in the behind with his boot or hit them in the face with his fist or a club."

In May 1940, Arnold Strippel married a woman who was just as Aryan and Germanic as himself. From June 1942 he continued his bloody trail at Majdanek concentration camp, where he was quickly promoted to *Untersturmführer* (second lieutenant). Next came Ravensbrück, then Peenemünde labor camp, followed by Herzogenbusch concentration camp in Vught, Holland. After a short stint at Drütte concentration camp, he was promoted again and, as an SS *Obersturmführer* (lieutenant), took command of all subcamps of Neuengamme concentration camp, in Hamburg. During the night of 20-21 April 1945 – only few days before the end of the war – twenty Jewish children were brutally murdered in one of the satellite camps under his command, in the basement of a former school on Bullenhuser Damm. The youngest were just 5 years old, the older ones 12. SS doctors had already carried out medical experiments on the children, having injected them with tuberculosis bacteria and operated on their lymph glands. The unscrupulous doctors did not see the children as human beings, but merely experimental material. As the Allied troops moved ever closer to Hamburg, all traces of the act were to be covered up. Thus, the twenty-eight adult prisoners who had been assigned to look after the children, and were therefore aware of what had taken place, were murdered in another satellite camp under Strippel's command. After this, the perpetrators removed their bloody uniforms and went into hiding. Including Strippel.

On 31 May 1946, the British Brigadier H. Shapcott brought charges against Strippel and two other SS perpetrators before the military court in Hamburg for the "killing of twenty children at the Bullenhuser Damm", but he had to do so without Strippel. Having first hidden with an SS friend near Rendsburg, Strippel later sought refuge as a farm worker in Hesse. In the autumn of 1948, when former SS leaders in West Germany felt safe again after the denazification procedure made it possible for countless Nazi perpetrators to return to bourgeois life, Arnold Strippel turned himself in under his real name at the American internment camp in Darmstadt. Without further ado, he received his proper papers and was released.

But at 2 pm on 13 December 1948, Strippel's past caught up with him for the first time. A Buchenwald prisoner, who Strippel had previously sentenced to hang from the notorious oak tree at the camp, recognized his former tormentor in Frankfurt's city center. The man called the police and Strippel was arrested.

His trial began on 31 May 1949 before a jury in Frankfurt. Strippel was accused not only of committing countless serious physical injuries to prisoners at Buchenwald, but of also being involved in the shooting of twenty-one Jewish prisoners, who had been murdered on 9 November in revenge for the bomb attack on Hitler in Munich's *Bürgerbräukeller*. The attack, planned and carried out by the journeyman carpenter Georg Elser, failed. Countless other reprisal killings were carried out by the Nazis as a deterrent and in revenge for the eight Hitler supporters who died in the assassination attempt, including at Buchenwald. According to the prosecution, on the order to "march", the "prisoners scattered outwards". Each SS man then shot the prisoner assigned to him.

Strippel denied his involvement, saying in court that he did not participate in the shootings because the matter was "too emotionally exhausting" for him.

Former prisoner Walter Poller had a completely different recollection of Strippel's role in the murders, as he reported in his 1946 memoir, *Arztschreiber in Buchenwald* (*A Doctor's Clerk in Buchenwald*):

> *Shortly after 10 am, Hauptscharführer Strippel called me by telephone. His voice sounded rough and drunk: "Well, do you know where the twenty-one shitheads are?"*
>
> *I didn't really know what to answer. Although I was in no doubt about the fate of the Jews, and also knew that you had to take what the Hauptscharführer said with a pinch of salt, the tone of his voice was so horrible that I quickly decided to feign ignorance.*
>
> *And then Strippel dictated twenty-one prisoner numbers and twenty-one names to me over the telephone. I went to the file and drew out twenty-one cards, wrote twenty-one death reports, and twenty-one times wrote down the cause of death: "Shot while trying to escape."'*
>
> *The next day I saw the corpses in the barracks.*

Strippel denied any involvement in the shooting. His denial, however, did not help him and on 1 June 1949, the court handed down its verdict: Strippel was sentenced to twenty-one life sentences "for twenty-one counts of murder". On top of that, he received another ten years in prison for serious bodily harm "in an indefinite number of cases".

He was sent to Butzbach Prison, 40 kilometers north of Frankfurt. Here he became an odd job man for the prison doctor and, not least because of his self-confident, often harsh demeanor, soon had considerable influence among the other prisoners and guards. He told the officials that he had merely done his duty in the concentration camps, nothing else. And they empathized with him.

The imprisoned Nazi criminals, including Strippel and the Frankfurt Gestapo chief Heinrich Baab, could not complain about the officials' lack of understanding anyway. On 20 April, Hitler's birthday, the group were able to celebrate undisturbed. Indeed, on that very day, Strippel had the opportunity to remember the incidents that marked the end of his cruel SS career: 20 April was the day on which the twenty Jewish children were murdered in the basement at Bullenhuser Damm. Strippel, however, did not want to remember anything. Least of all his participation.

"Today is the first time I have heard of an execution that allegedly took place in the basement of the school on Bullenhuser Damm. I had not received orders from any authority for this execution, nor had I passed on orders to my subordinates. I can no longer say where I was on the night of 20-21 April 1945," he said on the record on 10 May 1965, when an investigator from the public prosecutor's office in Butzbach sat opposite him.

The statement by four SS men involved in the crime claiming he also took part in the hanging of the children was considered by Strippel to be a conspiracy. "The only way I can explain it is that each of the accused had every conceivable interest in shifting the blame for the killing of the children onto me," he said of the allegations. The public prosecutor's office accepted his claim and discontinued the investigation.

Shortly thereafter, the Frankfurt jury concluded the Buchenwald trial in Strippel's favor. One of the prosecution's witnesses had been described as "generally unreliable" in another trial. Although the witness was only a marginal figure in Strippel's trial, the judiciary granted him a discount on his sentence, whereby the ten years he was due to serve for serious bodily harm "in an indefinite number of cases" was reduced to five years. The life sentences remained. The twenty-one dead

Jews from Buchenwald could not be pleaded away. Nevertheless, Arnold Strippel managed to pull off another coup: a retrial was once again permitted on the basis that Strippel may not have acted "as a fanatical National Socialist" in the collective murders, as the first verdict had so far assumed. First, the arrest warrant was revoked and Strippel left Butzbach Prison on 21 April 1969. As a man with a shady past, he did not have to worry about such existential things in Germany, and he quickly found a new job working as a bookkeeper for a Frankfurt business. A conscientious worker, the company was satisfied with its new accountant.

The process of the retrial then followed, which like so many other Nazi proceedings, dragged on and on. Former prisoners – insofar as they had survived the camps – often found it difficult to remember details, and the defense lawyers knew how to use this in their client's interest. After five months, the court finally announced the verdict of the retrial: it was still clear that Strippel was involved in the shooting of the twenty-one Jewish prisoners on 9 November. However, the Frankfurt judges Seiboldt, Steffgen and Dr Zander regarded him as being merely an "assistant", and for that sentenced him to six years in prison, to be served at Butzbach. Strippel would also receive compensation for his imprisonment of 121,500 marks. This was a lot of money at the time, amounting to seven times as much as his concentration camp prisoners would have received as compensation for the same amount of time, had they managed to escape from Strippel.

During questions in the Bundestag, the SPD member for parliament, Norbert Gansel, spoke for many when he asked: "How does the Federal Government judge that the former SS *Obersturmführer* and concentration camp guard Strippel. . . receive compensation for being imprisoned of 120,000 DM, while victims of Nazi tyranny only received compensation of 5 DM per day of imprisonment; and will the Federal Government initiate an amendment to the Federal Compensation Act with the aim of ensuring that victims of Nazi tyranny are not discriminated against in this macabre way against their tormentors?"

State Secretary Hermsdorf, on the other hand, argued against this during questions in the Bundestag on 9 May 1973: "The compensation paid to the concentration camp guard Strippel related only to material damage such as loss of earnings, reimbursement of social security contributions and expenses incurred in criminal proceedings. . .Given the extent of the damage and the number of victims, the damage caused by the loss of freedom could neither be completely balanced nor fully settled."

Arnold Strippel cared little about the parliamentary questions or public debates. He was now a wealthy citizen and bought a comfortable condominium in Frankfurt-Kalbach. What's more, the ex-SS *Obersturmführer* knew how to protect his property and his rights. When trees were due to be planted behind his house, he appeared at a meeting of the local advisory board. One of the participants remembers: "A tall, strapping man, loud and self-confident. He complained that the trees would shade his balcony." In the end, the trees were planted far away from Strippel's apartment.

But even in his bourgeois condominium, he could not escape the past. In November 1975, he and thirteen other concentration camp henchmen were once again on trial. This time in Düsseldorf, for crimes committed at Majdanek.

Majdanek was the name given to the concentration camp set up by the Waffen-SS 5 kilometers east of the Polish city of Lublin. How many people died there in the gas chambers, or were shot or beaten to death, no one knows, although historians estimate 350,000 lost their lives. More than 1,500 SS criminals and concentration camp guards carried out their murderous service here, with only a few of them being tried after the end of the war, let alone being convicted. The courts showed little interest in prosecuting the Majdanek criminals, despite a wealth of incriminating evidence provided by the Poles.

Public prosecutors spent twelve years investigating. Initially there were forty-seven accused, but this was then reduced down to fourteen. The rest were left in the all-too-complicated mesh of the German judiciary system.

When the presiding judge Günter Boden opened the trial in Room L 111 of the Düsseldorf Regional Court, he had no idea that it would become one of the longest in the Federal Republic of Germany's history: the verdicts would not be announced until May 1981. He also could not know that this five-year trial, this years-long dispute over perpetrators and actions, about guilt and punishment, would become more of a symbol for German jurisprudence than of making the reality and scale of the "Lublin Death Factory" known to the world.

Arnold Strippel was also in the dock on the opening day of the trial. The allegation: in July 1942 he was said to have been involved in the killing of forty-two Soviet prisoners of war at Majdanek. Of course, once again, Strippel denied everything.

He sat in the dock with a somber expression, at times shielding his eyes with dark sunglasses and giving the impression that it was all very boring and had nothing to do with him. On the 337th day of the trial, 6 June 1979, there was a commotion in the courtroom when Strippel unintentionally took center stage. In the audience were eleven Frenchmen, members of the association "Sons and Daughters of Deported Jews from France", who were following the trial. Among them was the Parisian dentist Henri Morgenstern. His father was murdered in Dachau, and his cousin Jacqueline was hanged on 20 April 1945 in the basement of the Hamburg elementary school on Bullenhuser Damm. She was just 12 years old. The man in charge of the murder operation was Arnold Strippel.

"Nazi murderer, Nazi murderer!", the group chanted, pointing at Strippel. The room stewards intervened as the judges left the room, as did some of the accused and their lawyers. Strippel remained demonstratively seated. Henri Morgenstern stood in front of him and, with tremendous excitement, began to speak, in German: "We are here because we are the children of the victims you executed. We owe the fact that we are still alive today to a true miracle. It's almost unbelievable that any of us can still be here to protest today, because almost all Jews were executed. . .Look at Strippel, this murderer who doesn't dare look me in the face, a coward, a child murderer! He hanged my little cousin Jacqueline Morgenstern. Look at this killer lowering his head!"

"A scene from the Old Testament," is how Günther Schwarberg later described these moments in his book *Der Juwelier von Majdanek* (*The Jeweler of Majdanek*), a rousing contemporary document in which he described the life and death of the Jewish jeweler Samuel Antmann and his family in the Majdanek concentration camp.

After the day of turmoil, the trial quickly returned to normality. An unbearable normality. While former prisoners remembered the horrors of Majdanek with often tearful agitation, the accused, seemingly unimpressed, sat on their benches and either talked to their lawyers, read newspapers, or dozed off – as if what was happening there had nothing to do with them. When they were called upon to justify themselves, they did so monotonically: "I was only following orders" or "I can't remember that anymore". No one wanted to remember. No one felt guilty. No one knew anything.

Strippel's behavior was no different than his co-defendants'. "I was just following orders from my superiors," he said, declaring the whole process to be a "gross injustice", a show trial. Some of the defense lawyers seemed to share the same opinion as their clients, trying by any means possible to hinder proceedings. Time and again they questioned the credibility of the witnesses. "Equal to zero" was their probative value, which was all lawyer Stratmann could say without receiving a reprimand from the judge.

On 26 June 1981, the defense lawyers made their pleas, with all of them demanding acquittals for their clients. Strippel also made his closing words: "I am completely innocent," he said. And: "In my life, I have always stood up for everything I have done."

In their closing statement, the prosecution considered Strippel to be a "person who could be used for any purpose". On 30 June 1981, visibly nervous and with a moving voice, Richter Bogen announced the verdicts:

- *Hermine Ryan-Braunsteiner, two counts of murder: life imprisonment.*
- *Hildegard Lächert, aiding and abetting in the murder of 100 people: twelve years imprisonment.*
- *Hermann Hackmann, aiding and abetting in the murder of 141 people and the execution of 200 to 400 ill persons: ten years imprisonment.*
- *Emil Laurich, aiding and abetting in five counts of murder: eight years imprisonment.*
- *Heinz Villain, aiding and abetting in two murders, assisting in the murder of 18,000 people and taking part in the selection of 1,500 people: six years imprisonment.*
- *Fritz Heinrich Petrick, aiding and abetting in 41 counts of murder: four years imprisonment.*
- *Thomas Ellwanger, aiding and abetting in 100 counts of murder: three years imprisonment.*
- *Heinrich Groffmann: acquitted.*

And Arnold Strippel? He was sentenced to 3 years and six months in prison for being an accessory to 41 counts of murder.

After the verdict was announced, a storm of protest broke out in the courtroom. Shouts of "Scandal!", "Shame!", and "Unbelievable!" could be heard in the auditorium. Once peace had been restored, Judge Bogen spent eleven long hours justifying the verdicts. Regarding Strippel, he explained that "no excesses had been reported. . ." and although he had been sentenced to several years in prison, he could go home that evening as a free man. The arrest warrant had been overturned and Strippel could now be sure that he would not have to atone for his murderous deeds in Majdanek. He had lawyers, doctors, and all the necessary documentation, and so returned to his accustomed life as a well-off pensioner in his condominium in Kalbach.

The trial had come to an end. A scandalous trial. A German trial. The defense lawyer for an accused SS guard was elected carnival prince by the Düsseldorf Carnival Association; an elderly woman, who had been particularly committed to taking care of one of the accused SS guards during the trial, received the Order of Merit from the Federal Republic of Germany from President Carstens for her "self-sacrificing work"; finally, a former SS *Unterscharführer* called Heinrich Groffmann, a sadistic thug from Behringen whom witnesses described as being particularly cruel and who had been accused of murdering 17,102 people, walked out of the courtroom a free man.

And even in the case of the gruesome murder of the twenty Jewish children in Hamburg, Strippel had no need to fear that the judiciary would disturb his tranquil life as a pensioner. Relatives filed further complaints, but the wheels of the German judiciary grind slowly – as is so often the case when it comes to Nazi perpetrators. Before a new lawsuit could take place, the judges wanted to know whether Strippel was even capable of standing trial. The answer was provided by three renowned Frankfurt experts on request. Their diagnosis: Not able to stand trial. A neurology expert, Professor Fischer, certified that Strippel was a "multimorbid patient". His colleague, Professor Schöppe, senior physician of internal medicine, who saved Strippel from imprisonment after the Majdanek verdict in a report dated 17 September 1985 (diagnosis: "unfit to be imprisoned"), once again agreed that he was "unable to stand trial".

Spring 1992: I am back in Kalbach. The curtains in Strippel's window are drawn. Despite repeatedly ringing the bell, no one opens. I walk over to the neighboring houses. The front gardens are all well-kept, presenting an orderly terraced-house idyll. I ring the bells and sometimes a door opens. Arnold Strippel? "No, there's nothing to say about that; I have no opinion." Doors are closed, sometimes in a friendly, embarrassed way, but mostly jerkily, accompanied by a brief, often loud and aggressive, comment: "Get out of here, quickly!"

Only Frau R. lets me in. An hour later, having told her about her neighbor's career in the concentration camps, she seems perplexed and depressed. She knew nothing about it. The murder of the Jewish children leaves her speechless for a while. "But with everything that's happened," she says later, pulling her little daughter close to her, "at some point there has to be peace." Peace for the perpetrators?

Years later, in the autumn, I am back in Kalbach searching for clues. The name Strippel can no longer be found on the doorbell on Talstraße. The neighbors only vaguely remember the old man with the robust appearance. "Strippel? No, there's no one here of that name," says a young woman, briskly. "He died a few years ago," says an older man in a broad Hessian dialect.

His grave cannot be found in the cemetery behind the small church.

A DEATH SENTENCE
OR: THE SECOND CAREER OF ROLAND FREISLER

Friday, 17 November 1944. At around 10 am, a closed van brought 21-year-old Margot von Schade from Berlin's Moabit prison to the People's Court at Bellevuestraße. Inside, she sat silently across from two women: 23-year-old Barbara Sensfuß and 40-year-old Käthe Törber. All three had been charged with the "undermining of military morale". The court hearing was due to begin in a couple of hours. What would happen to them? What did they expect?

Von Schade and the two other women had only been told that morning that the trial was taking place. Now, on the drive through Berlin's streets, which she could only see vaguely through the windscreen over the driver's shoulder, she felt miserable. And alone. She thought about her family: her mother, stepfather, sister. Where were they now? She was afraid.

An hour later: A large hall with chalky white walls. In front of the judge's bench were three chairs for the accused. Next to them, lined up left and right, were uniformed guards. They were intimidating: "There is no escape here," their faces seem to say. At the front of the hall – from floor to ceiling– a blood-red swastika flag hung conspicuously. In front of it, on a narrow pedestal, was a bronze bust of Hitler.

Margot von Schade stared hypnotized at the huge red cloth. It looked threatening to her. She took a quick look at the spectator benches. An anonymous mas of brown and black uniforms. She heard a muffled murmur of voices. Everything remained shadowy, unreal.

"All rise" – the military tone of command from one of the guards penetrated the courtroom. Suddenly there was calm. The door to the side of the judge's bench opened. The court entered. Red robes, red berets, grey and black uniforms – the assessors. First of all, the chairman: Freisler. She looked him straight in the face. Their eyes met for a moment. He glanced at his wristwatch. The trial began.

Margot von Schade followed the tribunal as if in a trance. Later, when she could no longer remember how much time had passed, she jumped up with a start: "Von Schade! Stand up!" Freisler's cutting voice was unmistakable. He read out the indictment point by point. No, he did not read, it was a single roar. After the "mean and devious assassination attempt on our leader on 20 July," he said, full of pathos and with great theatrical gestures, the defendant made publicly corrosive statements. After the special report on "the miraculous salvation of the Führer" had been broadcast on the radio, the defendant had made the following derogatory statement: "Unlucky." What's more, the "criminal officers who carried out the attack," the accused publicly remarked, "were not cowards but, on the contrary, had shown courage".

A murmur of horror rippled through the rows of spectators and grew louder when Freisler, his voice trembling with indignation, quoted a phrase from the indictment that must have appeared to every staunch National Socialist to be a paragon of depravity: "A fucking *Gefreiter* [private first class]", that's what this depraved girl called the Führer – "unbelievable!" Freisler was beside himself, his fanatical gaze aimed at Margot von Schade. She looked down. How was she supposed to counter this slobbering monologue? How was she to be heard? How could she defend herself? When she did manage to break through Freisler's tirade, she was harshly rebuked after just a few sentences. Was there no one there in the courtroom to help her? Where was her lawyer? Margot von Schade felt powerless. Defeated. Abandoned.

Earlier, she had wanted to say so much when the two co-defendants appeared, who in this case were also appearing as witnesses against her. She wanted to tell them how it really was, to describe what had actually happened back then, following the radio report on 20 July. But Freisler had prevented her from speaking. Now, just a few steps away from her, sat the two women who had once been her confidants, but who had now shifted all the blame onto her. They wanted to save their own skins, nothing more. Margot von Schade sensed that any sort of denunciation would be welcome at this tribunal. A lesson for everyone in the hall, so that they could see and experience what happened to someone who placed themselves outside the "national community". Just like in the age of witch hunts, she thought. Now I'm the witch here. Ready to burn. . .

At some point, she had long since grown tired and could no longer follow the macabre spectacle but could still hear the monotonous voice of her lawyer. Their closing speech sounded routine, indifferent. But were they really "her" lawyer? No, this woman did not have her trust. They had only spoken once – and only for a few minutes – before the trial, back in the detention center. This lawyer knew nothing about her, did not want to know anything about her. To her she was just a "case" like many others, a "file number". Nothing else. She had been hired by the court as a public defender. And she did her duty, as was expected of her.

Now that the tribunal was coming to an end, Margot von Schade sensed how much danger she was in. In the past few hours, she had experienced how her two co-defendants were treated by the court as being "seduced" but had been "essentially" honest comrades of the people; how their lawyers presented exculpatory arguments, and how even Freisler managed to find sympathetic words for the pair's behavior.

It was quite different with her. From the start she was met with Freisler's irritated questions. Why? Because she was of noble birth? After 20 July was anyone with "von" in their name automatically a co-conspirator with the Stauffenbergs? Did she suffer from Freisler's wrath because her answers lacked the insight he ruefully expected of her?

Such thoughts flew around her head. Did Freisler not say earlier in a cynical tone: "This is the sort of family, the environment from which the accused comes"? Had he not drooled in mock indignation: "Tell me who you're working with – and I'll tell you who you are." Everything had been used against her, even the letter her sister Gisela had sent to her prison cell and which, of course, had been intercepted by the officials and immediately used as incriminating evidence. In the letter, Gisela had reported on a social gathering, where there would have been drinking and dancing. Yet Freisler saw this once again as proof of her decadent family background. A background that meant everything, not just in the way it benefitted a "good" German in these difficult times.

This young Margot von Schade, this rebellious brat, who had dared to publicly insult the Führer in the "most shameless way", who even regretted the assassination attempt's failure with her subversive remarks – a deterrent example had to be made of this vile person.

The court withdrew to deliberate, but had everything not already been decided? Depressed, strangely agitated, Margot von Schade sat in her chair. Time seemed to stand still. She felt like she was in a vacuum.

At some point she lost all sense of time, but soon the judges and assessors reentered the hall to proclaim their judgment. Freisler's cutting voice was unmistakable:

"Sensfuß – stand up! Acquitted! Törber – stand up! Acquitted!"

Hope started to rise up in her. If her two co-defendants had been acquitted, perhaps she can just get away with a prison sentence. . .

"Von Schade – stand up!"

Her eyes looked ahead: red robe, red flag, the bust of the Führer. . .

"I sentence you to death for undermining military morale, for favoring the enemy, for your defeatist statements and for treason!"

"The death sentence?" she thought. "For me? This cannot be. I am not a criminal, not a murderer."

While Freisler read out the reasons behind his decision, she tried to process the enormous scope of what had happened. The death penalty? Could it all end just like that? All because of a frivolous comment in a friendly setting? The two other women were there as well, they laughed and joked. Why had they been acquitted? Why should she be killed?

The death penalty for such a thing – impossible! She looked for her stepfather's face, knowing that he was somewhere in the audience. "Is it real? Is it true? Should I, do I have to die? Is 17 November really my fateful day? Is there just the guillotine waiting for me?"

Margot von Schade, now Margot Diestel, survived. The premature end of the "Thousand Year Reich" saved her life. Thanks to the Russians' advance, the execution never took place. As a death row inmate, she had survived the air raids in her prison cell and the agonizing transfer from Berlin to the prison in Stolpen, Saxony, where, in the last days of the war, a courageous guard refused orders to shoot the inmates before the approaching enemy arrived. Instead, when the Russian troops were already in front of the city, he issued release certificates: "Margot von Schade will be released today." Stamp, signature, date. It was 3 May 1945.

Four days later, *Generaloberst* Jodl signed the German surrender in the western French city of Reims. The war was over.

Twenty-four years later, Margot von Schade – one of the few who escaped – began to write her life story. Her childhood, the denunciation, her arrest, the death sentence at the People's Court, her grueling prison ordeal, the constant fear of death, she was determined to tell her grandchildren everything. They needed to know what had happened in Germany. Almost inadvertently, her story became a moving historical document. The memories of these horror years – recorded by her husband, Arnold Diestel – found a publisher. The book should, she writes, "open the eyes of the next generation". Because: "What happened once must never happen again."

In retrospect, Margot Diestel does not see herself as a resistance fighter. But at a young age she recognized what National Socialism was doing to Germany and to the world. "As a 21-year-old girl in the peaceful city of Demnin, knowing things, suspecting things, being filled with disgust at this criminal system, led to a few cheeky comments. It was as if we were living in perfect peace, as if there were no denunciations, no Gestapo and no concentration camps – that's how I pushed my opinion in everyone's face," she recalls. Her carelessness almost cost her her life – in the name of the German people. She published the original justification in her memoir.

IN THE NAME OF THE GERMAN PEOPLE!

In the criminal case against Margot von Schade from Demmin, born on 27 March 1923 in Castle Zievrich

due to undermining of military morale

the People's Court, 1st Senate, responded to the indictment received on 30 October 1944 from the Reich Attorney at the main hearing of 17 November 1944, in which the following judges took part:

President of the People's Court Dr Freisler, Chairman

District Court Director Dr Schlemann,

SA-*Brigadeführer* Hauer,

NSKK-*Obergruppenführer* Government
Director Offermann,

Deputy Gauleiter Simon, as a representative of the Reich
AttorneyThe District Court of Zeschau hereby rules:

Margot von Schade glorified the assassins of 20 July,
regretted the failure of the assassination attempt on
the Führer,
sought to bring shame on our Führer, and, shamelessly,
talked "politically" with a Russian.

Forever dishonored, she is punished with death.

Justifications:

.

.

She admitted that she commented on the assassination,
saying: "Unlucky!", unlucky that the assassination attempt
was unsuccessful!!

.

.

That alone removes her from our midst. For we want
nothing, nothing at all, in common with someone who
declares his solidarity with traitors to the people, Führer
and Reich, who through their betrayal would have sent us
directly into shame and death if they had succeeded.
Margot von Schade, however, and this may be noted
as a complete picture of her depravity, made her mean
statements on the basis of a thoroughly treacherous,
dishonorable attitude.

.

.

No wonder, as she herself admits, when she and her comrades went to the community reception of the Führer's address, she declared:

"Mr. Hitler speaks!" Everyone must be angry and ashamed that a German girl, in 1944, could express herself in that way.

·

·

Anyone who, in such shameless, self-abasement as a German, conducts such conversations with a Bolshevik, who glorifies the meanest betrayal of our history in such a way, who tries to make our Führer contemptible in this way, thereby defiles our entire people.

For reasons of purity, we no longer wish to have anything to do with someone who has atomized their whole personality in such a way, destroying it forever.

Anyone who spreads this subversion in this way, who thus makes themselves a stooge of our wartime enemies, must pay with death, because we must, at all costs, protect the staunch position of our homeland and our people who are struggling hard for their lives.

·

·

Because Margot von Schade has been convicted, she must also bear the costs.

Dr Freisler   Dr Schlemann

Forty-six years later, in Steinhorst, near Hamburg, I am sitting opposite the woman whom Freisler had sentenced to death in Berlin.

How does it feel today, when reading your own death sentence? Does she feel angry, does she have feelings of revenge? "No," says Margot von Schade (now Diestel), shaking her head, "only paralysis and disappointment. Almost all the judges of the People's Court returned to office after the war. No one has been held accountable or convicted, and that is depressing."

The fact is those perpetrators of violence dressed in red robes were never brought to justice. Apart from a few tiresome and impotent admonishments, no one in post-war Germany urged people to confront the murders and unjust verdicts of the Nazi judiciary. Least of all the judiciary itself.

Only from time to time were there lawyers who did not adhere to the general *esprit de corps*, including former Berlin Senator Gerhard Meyer. During his term of office, a later (and final) attempt to come to terms with the past was made by the Attorney General at the Berlin Court of Appeal in October 1979. Investigations were resumed against seventy-four surviving former members of the People's Court, including eleven judges, forty-eight prosecutors and fifteen honorary judges. Yet it was clear from the start that the point was not to state that almost all the death sentences handed down at the People's Court had nothing to do with an independent jury, but were simply one thing: crimes.

Seven years later, in October 1986, the investigations against the lawyers of the Nazi Death Tribunal were finally dropped. It was thus clear that all 5,243 death sentences handed down by Hitler's judges would remain unpunished.

Meyer's successor, the CDU man Rupert Scholz, considered the fact that there would be no trial against these former judges to be "unsatisfactory and very regrettable for anyone who believes in justice". Beautiful, reassuring words for what is a German disgrace, in which politics and the judiciary were equally involved.

The People's Court was a merciless death machine of the Nazis and a weapon in the persecution of opponents of the totalitarian system. From 1942 to 1945, the fanatical judges handed down an average of ten death sentences a day. German lawyers were masters of life and death.

"The People's Court will always try to pass judgement as it believes that you, my Führer, would judge the case yourself," VGH President Freisler wrote to Hitler.

A death sentence handed down on 14 October 1943 may prove what he meant by this. One judgement in thousands; an exemplary "German judgment":

IN THE NAME OF THE GERMAN PEOPLE!

In the criminal case against the postal worker Georg Jurkowski from Berlin-Weißensee, born in Berlin on 31 July 1891, currently in custody for the following offence:

The undermining of military morale

As decided by the 1st Senate of the People's Court on the basis of the main hearing of 14 October 1943, in which the following judges took part:

President of the People's Court Dr Freisler, Chairman
Chairman of the *Kammergerichtsrat* Rehse
Gauhauptstellenleiter Mayor Ahmels
Ortsgruppenleiter Kelch
Kreisleiter Reinecke, representative of the
Oberreichsanwalt
First Public Prosecutor Domann

hereby rule:
At the beginning of August, Georg Jurkowski made subversive and defeatist statements on a street in Danzig [Gdansk], saying in particular that the Führer would be like Mussolini, and would no longer be alive by January. Forever dishonored, he is punished with death for being a propagandist for our wartime enemies.

Justifications:

Georg Jurkowski works as a postman in the railway service and as such was in Danzig on 3 August with fellow postal worker Schönherr from Berlin, who also worked on the railway. He wanted to return to Berlin at around 10.30 am. At 10 am he went to the Stockturm tower with Schönherr, in the direction of the train station. By chance, our compatriot Rosemarie Grande was walking behind them and quite clearly heard Jurkowski tell Schönherr that Hermann Göring had acquired a sixth property in Italy, having enriched himself with foreign property owned by others. When she heard this, she caught up and confronted Jurkowski, while Schönherr, believing that she must be an acquaintance, carried on walking and did not hear the rest. Grande told Jurkowski not to trumpet his statements like that, but to keep them to himself. Jurkowski replied: "Miss, you will think differently about it in two months. All I can tell you is that il Duce is under arrest, and it will soon be the same for Hitler. He won't be alive in January." Inwardly deeply affected by these statements, in order to be better able stand up to Jurkowski, our compatriot Grande now said that she was with the Gestapo.
Jurkowski replied:
"Well, if you're with the Gestapo then you'll know even more than I do, and afterwards you'll be even worse off than us."
Grande looked for a police officer and after finding one, located Jurkowski and Schönherr at a tram stop. As soon as Jurkowski saw her with the officer, he fled. However, he was confronted by passers-by and taken to the police station. As he sat there with Grande, he told her: "You can have anything you want from me. Here's my watch, but just let me go."

All of this was stated today in the utmost certainty by the witness Rosemarie Grande, just as she did before the police. She makes an impeccable impression, and the People's Court is convinced that she said not a word too little or too much. There are no discrepancies, even down to the street noise Jurkowski refers to.

Jurkowski denies having made those statements. Of course, when confronted he said that the people's compatriot Grande would experience something in two months' time, but by that he meant our retaliatory attacks, even if he had not said so at the time. And before that, he had only talked to Schönherr about wanting to visit a castle – he now says Neuhaus in Franconia – but that this was not possible because the *Reichsmarschall* had been there. He made no threats against Grande because of her alleged affiliation with the Gestapo (in reality she is an employee of the Reich Governor).

But Jurkowski's guilty conscience was proven when he ran away, which he inadequately explains was otherwise due to concern that he would miss his train, which even Schönherr, who appears as a witness today, was also extremely surprised about. And offering her his watch at the police station, when he could no longer catch the train, was also a poor attempt by Jurkowski to explain his intention to avoid inconvenience. His guilty conscience is therefore clear.

Even so, the testimony of our compatriot Grande gives the People's Court the certainty that it happened as she said it did; even without the need for Schönherr's witness statement and his testimony, who, as he says, could not really hear anything anyway because when he was talking with Jurkowski, he was separated from him every now and again by the traffic, and also paid no attention to his speeches because they did not interest him.

We must thank our compatriot Rosemarie Grande for her decisive and correct intervention. In doing so, she acted as a German citizen ought to act today. She has exposed a dangerous, defeatist, corrosive agitator, who has broken his oath to the Führer in such a shameful manner. Anyone who acts like this at the end of the fourth year of the war shows that he is devoid of all honor. Therefore, in order to protect our inner unity, he must be permanently dishonored and punished with death.

Because Jurkovsky has been convicted, he must also bear the costs.

Signed
Dr Freisler   Rehse

Freisler and Rehse; two merciless German judges. Two violent criminals in robes. Two exemplary perpetrators.

Freisler's piercing voice and threatening gestures still sometimes haunt Frau Diestel's dreams, robbing her of sleep. It is as if this greedy, screaming master of life and death is still passing judgment over people today. A merciless Nazi lawyer, who was one of the outstanding pioneers of Nazi injustice, had a very "German" career:

Dr Roland Freisler, who began his career as a lawyer in Kassel, joined the NSDAP in 1925 and was a member of the Prussian state parliament in 1932. After the National Socialists seized power, he was first the Ministerial Director and later State Secretary at the Prussian Ministry of Justice and a member of the NSDAP parliamentary group in the Reichstag. A fanatical National Socialist, he had formulated his ideas for a National Socialist People's Court as early as 1934.

He published his ideas in an article for the *Zeitschrift der Akademie für Deutsches Recht* (*Journal for the Academy of German Law*): "Charges must be brought within twenty-four hours. . .

the verdict within another twenty-four, and the criminal must face his punishment immediately. The era of mitigating circumstances as a rule must be over. . ."

After the dissolution of the Prussian Ministry of Justice, Freisler was appointed State Secretary in the Reich Ministry of Justice on 1 April 1934. Here, too, he was quickly regarded as the absolute guarantor of National Socialist sentiment, and now headed the department for the area of law that was particularly important to the party: criminal law. In addition, there was the organization of the judiciary and – Freisler's greatest challenge – the People's Court. The National Socialists subordinated the judiciary completely to the objectives of their policies. Step by step, the still valid Civil Code was substantially amended and robbed of its original content. Under the pretext of protecting the interests of the people and the State, criminal law in particular became a form of martial law under the National Socialists.

State Secretary Dr Freisler was always at the forefront of the battle, tirelessly putting down on paper what he considered legally and ideologically necessary for the defense of the "most sacred German values". A particular concern was always the People's Court. It was clear to him that this court had to assume the leading role within the entire German judiciary. Freisler attributed the confusion that was characteristic of the judiciary before 1933 primarily to lack of orientation, which should now come to an end.

In the People's Court, the idea of leadership should be realized in a special way, as an exemplary illustration for all subordinate German courts. The president of every State senate must be the leader, whose instructions were to be followed by professional and lay judges without question. Only in this way could a "Germanic" form of negotiation be possible, a vision he developed in an essay published in 1935. The judge alone would bear responsibility, his task being to carry out the procedure as quickly as possible. At best, Freisler allowed lay judges to carry out an advisory role, nothing more. In a "Germanic court case", all those involved, from experienced judges to young lawyers, were "soldiers of the law".

Dr Roland Freisler saw himself as a "political soldier" and described himself thus in a letter he sent to Hitler on 15 October 1942, following his appointment as President of the People's Court. The most bloodthirsty era of the Nazi tribunals began with Freisler and continued until his death on 3 February 1945.

On that day, the American Air Force carried out its heaviest attack on Berlin to date, in which 700 bombers, accompanied by fighter planes, dropped over 3,000 tons of explosives on the city, killing more than 20,000 people. Victims of a cruel war that was now returning to where it had begun: the very center of National Socialism. Among the victims was Roland Freisler.

For a long time, there were three versions of his end. The first came from Fabian von Schlabrendorff, the man who was the last defendant to stand before Freisler and who was to survive the war. Later, he recalled the events of 3 February 1945 in a book, stating that shortly after the start of the main hearing against him, the alarm sirens sounded and they proceeded to the basement of the courthouse. The President, with files in hand, and his assessors would have stood in one corner of the shelter. In the other was von Schlabrendorff and the team of guards. Suddenly, the building was hit by a heavy bomb and a ceiling beam broke through, killing Freisler.

According to the second version of events, Freisler was said to have been hit by a bomb while driving from the Reich Ministry of Justice to the People's Court.

The third, and most likely version, proceeded as follows: The Chief Medical Officer Dr Rolf Schleicher was on his way to see Reich Minister of Justice Thierack to intervene on behalf of his brother, Rüdiger Schleicher, who worked in the Reich Aviation Ministry. Freisler had sentenced him and Klaus Bonhoeffer, the brother of Pastor Dietrich Bonhoeffer, to death the day before, together with Friedrich Perels and Hans John. The bombing raid meant that Schleicher had to wait with many other passengers in the subway tunnel at Potsdamer Platz. He was accompanied by his sister-in-law and her daughter, who wanted to talk to Chief Prosecutor Lautz about the death sentence. When the bombing subsided and the deadly squadrons had finally left, a doctor was called for. Schleicher came forward and was taken to the courtyard of the nearby People's Court. Once there, he was shown a "high-ranking person" who had been hit by shrapnel while attempting to across the courtyard. The man was no longer alive. Schleicher bent down and looked the dead man in the face, only to see it was the same man who, a day earlier, had sentenced his brother to death: Roland Freisler.

He refused to issue a death certificate and demanded to see the Reich Minister of Justice. When he was finally able to talk to him, Thierack said he was very upset about Freisler's death, but promised Schleicher that he would first postpone his brother's execution. After submitting a petition for clemency, he hoped the verdict would be reviewed at a later date.

Unfortunately, all his efforts would be in vain. Weeks later, on the night of 22-23 April 1945, Rüdiger Schleicher and a further sixteen death row inmates were executed by a firing squad from the Reich Security Main Office. Among them were Bonhoeffer, John and Perels.

Freisler, the robed murderer, was dead. Three days later, on 5 February 1945, Reich Minister of Justice Georg Thierack wrote a letter of condolence to the grieving widow, "dear Frau Freisler":

It was with deep shock that I became aware of the heavy hand of fate that has struck you and your family. In the midst of restless activity, facing new difficult tasks, your husband has been recalled. The magnitude of the loss to the judiciary is already evident in the few hours that have passed since then.

A man full of ideas, a tireless worker, a National Socialist who was deeply convinced of the greatness of the German mission, of justice and of the victory of the German cause, and a faithful follower of the Führer has been torn from our midst with his passing. There is certainly a special tragedy in this, but at the same time it is also a symbol for the fulfillment of this militant life that your husband fell at his place of work, to which he had rushed during the attack out of a special sense of responsibility as President of the highest political court that had been entrusted to his leadership.

By expressing the condolences of the German judiciary to you, dear Frau Freisler, I would also like to assure you of my personal sympathy. May the thought that your husband lives on in your sons give you the strength to comfort you.

Heil Hitler! Your very devoted. . .

Thierack's signature followed. The press release distributed on the same day by the Reich Ministry of Justice press office, with a request to the editors to "refrain from further commenting on the above report and making their own additions to the newspapers", comprised only a few lines. Under the title "Dr Roland Freisler, fallen", the following was briefly reported:

During the terrorist attack on the Reich capital on 3 February, the President of the People's Court, NSKK-Brigadeführer Dr Roland Freisler, was killed. Dr Freisler, 52, had been a member of the NSDAP since 1925 and a recipient of the party's Golden Medal of Honor. He was a member of the German Reichstag and was a Prussian State Councilor. Dr Freisler was known to the widest circles of the German people as a tireless champion of National Socialist German law.

The Nuremberg Military Tribunal called Freisler "the darkest, most brutal and bloodiest judge of the entire German judiciary" and counted him, along with Himmler, Heydrich and Thierack, among those men "whose desperate and despicable characters were known to the world".

This assessment should not be contradicted. After 1945, Freisler was made the scapegoat of the German judiciary, as well as its alibi. The surviving Nazi lawyers used the demonization of Freisler to unload their own guilt on his back.

In this way they could feel like lawyers who, in difficult times, had simply done their duty, as the law demanded. It allowed them to see themselves as being seduced, as the victims, rather than as perpetrators and accomplices. Their guilty conscience – if they had one – could be quieted, their feelings of guilt transferred to others. A fanatical judge like Freisler was a particularly suitable person for them to project such feelings onto.

Freisler's fellow murderer, Hans-Joachim Rehse, survived the end of the war. In 1968 he stood before the Federal Court of Justice as a defendant. However, a lack of legal finesse meant his conviction failed. The BGH qualified Rehse "as a member of a collegial court" that was "according to the law in force at the time, independent, equal, subject only to the law and responsible to its own conscience".

His case was referred back to the lower court. Rehse, who was involved in 373 verdicts, including over 230 death sentences, died before the trial could finally be concluded.

Rehse fared the same as all the other lawyers at the Nazi death tribunal: none of the 106 professional judges and 179 prosecutors of the People's Court has ever been convicted, nor have any of the thousands of special or military judges. After the war, they could all count on the understanding of their fellow judges.

"The only way a judge who issues a death sentence can be liable to prosecution is if he bends the law. This presupposes that he consciously and intentionally violates procedural law or substantive law," the Federal Court of Justice ruled, thus issuing a blanket acquittal to the Nazi death judges. Which of them had confessed to having "consciously" and "intentionally" bent the law? No one felt guilty, so no one was charged.

So why the public outrage on the part of Berlin Justice Senator Scholz, when the VGH's past was finally filed away in 1968? Why was it surprising that the investigations by the Berlin judiciary – demanded and promoted by Scholz's predecessor, Meyer, in 1979 – ended in impunity for the accused?

Had there not been a trial for Rehse? Was there not already a sentence in the acquittal that claimed the People's Court was an "independent court subject only to the law"?

The absurd verdict of the Berlin Regional Court in 1986 merely continued the obscene logic of post-war justice as a whole. Was there ever even an interest in holding those responsible for the Nazi judiciary to account?

The mills of justice ground slowly; Nazi judges rarely got stuck in them. Until the 1960s, the judiciary was characterized by inertia and indifference when it came to addressing the past of its bloodstained peers.

After the founding of the Federal Republic of Germany, trials for manslaughter would still have been possible, but the statute of limitations for this expired in 1960. Now only criminal prosecution for murder was possible, but this presupposes that the defendant committed the act "for base motives". A Nazi judge who insisted on having only applied the "valid law" could not be proven to have had this motive. A committed Nazi judge had, not just from his own point of view, an honorable attitude, a view shared by the majority of post-war judges and politicians.

Thousands quickly changed their National Socialist dispositions and returned to German courtrooms as judges and prosecutors. Even the few Nazi colleagues whose disreputable past led to unpleasant public criticism could count on the caring nature of the new Adenauer state: they were released into retirement with a full pension as compensation.

"The decline of the law was not processed, but gilded," wrote *Der Spiegel*'s editor Rolf Lamprecht. Justice and politics worked hand in hand, acting as if nothing had ever happened.

Frau Diestel shakes her head when she thinks about how Germany's past was – and still is – suppressed. "Who among the young people knows about this catastrophe, who tells them?" she asks.

A German catastrophe and a German shame that hardly anyone wants to remember. Not the judiciary, not politicians. Certainly not the perpetrators and those who allowed their actions to take place.

Fate was kind to the fun-loving girl Margot von Schade and the respectable Frau Diestel. Later, but not too much later, she received compensation, at least in a very private way. She could not count on state reparations in Germany. She was a victim, not a perpetrator. And in Germany, state welfare was – and still is – more for the perpetrators than for the victims.

Months later, in June 1991, in a quiet, elegant Munich residential area, close to the Nymphenburg Canal, stands a modern block of flats containing eleven apartments. On the ground floor, to the left of the apartment door, is a simple cardboard sign: Russegger.

None of the neighbors knows that the old lady is Marion Freisler, the widow of the former President of the People's Court, Roland Freisler. "She's a very withdrawn woman, she hardly speaks to anyone," a resident tells me. Frau Russegger does not speak to me either. I had written a letter to her weeks before asking for an interview; how does she feel today about the merciless work of her husband, how did she explain the father to her two sons? That is what I wanted to ask her, and much more. My letter went unanswered. Now, in early summer, I am in Munich. A final – albeit unsuccessful – attempt.

During my research, I had come across press reports from 1958. At that time, a Berlin tribunal – the last in Germany – had imposed a fine of 100,000 marks on Freisler's estate. The sum corresponded to the value of two properties in Berlin, which had been under trusteeship since the end of the war, and which Freisler's widow now claimed as her property. For years she had fought to have the houses returned on the grounds that they had been bought by her dowry. The Berlin court, however, came to the conclusion that the acquisitions from Freisler's income benefitted his wife. In doing so, the board relied on the fact that the installment payments for the land, stretching over years, coincided with the dates of Freisler's salary payments and the stages of his career. Investigations had also revealed that Frau Freisler was originally penniless, and that there was therefore no dowry.

After a four-and-a-half-hour hearing, at which Freisler's widow had not appeared on the grounds that "she could not bear any exertion", the Chamber dismissed the appeal of Frau Russegger, her alias, who was living in Frankfurt at the time. The new fine, which was the same amount as the one already imposed by the Berlin court on 29 January 1958, corresponded to the value of the two properties, but now these would be confiscated instead of the money being taken.

Almost thirty years later, in February 1985, the widow, or more precisely her pension case, hit the headlines again. Günther Wirth, a member of the Bavarian SPD State Parliament, made public that after the war, Frau Russegger not only received the usual basic widow's pension from her husband's job (after he had died in a bombing raid on Berlin shortly before the end of the war), but, since 1974, had also received a so-called compensation pension, granted by the Munich Pension Office, on the grounds that it must be assumed Freisler – if he had survived the war – "would have worked as a lawyer or civil servant of the higher service".

This ludicrous argument caused a sensation at the time because it was only with this survival theory that the widow's claim to a virtually lost income or pension share could be justified at all. However, "for constitutional reasons", the Bavarian social security officials "could not take the view" that Freisler would have been sentenced "to death or at least to lifelong imprisonment" had he survived. Rather, it seemed to them "just as likely" that the supreme Nazi judge "would have continued to work in the profession he had trained for, or in another profession, especially since an amnesty or temporary occupational ban would also have been considered".

The *Süddeutsche Zeitung* commented at the time that anyone who could "invent, formulate and approve" such notifications, must "have the heart of a butcher's dog". The "Munich pension case" triggered fierce discussions in almost all major German newspapers. "How can anyone be a victim of war who wanted, promoted and prolonged the war?" asked Franz-Josef Müller, a

Munich Social Democrat who himself stood before Freisler in 1943, aged 18, as a member of the "White Rose" resistance group and had been sentenced by him to five years in prison.

Forty years after Freisler perished with the Third Reich, the case of Freisler's pension payment polarized opinions on how to deal with the country's Nazi past. A letter to the editor of the *Süddeutsche Zeitung* found it "shameful that there are people who have nothing else to do but rummage through old pension notices forty years after the end of the war". The writer was by no means alone in his opinion.

Robert M.W. Kempner, an American prosecutor at the Nuremberg Trials after the war, also spoke out in the same newspaper: "In addition to the war victims' pension and the damage compensation pension, the widow also receives a widow's pension from the social security system," he wrote. His detailed letter to the editor brought further explosive details to the public: "Freisler", he continued, "never paid social security contributions, because he was in receipt of his high judge's salary. She should not be able to receive a widow's pension, as such a pension is not granted if an official has behaved inhumanely. This follows from the provisions of Article 131 of the Basic Law. In such cases, however, a pension is only granted if the employer, i.e. the State, pays for the person concerned. For Freisler, since the widow receives social security, considerable sums must have been paid back by the State."

At the end of his letter to the editor, Kempner criticized the fact that Freisler was classified as the People's Court President in his widow's pension case and wrote that, in his opinion, he "should only have been classified as a gravedigger of the German judiciary, and therefore receive the normal salary of a gravedigger working in a cemetery".

Alarmed by the fierce public reaction, the then Bavarian Labor and Social Affairs Minister Franz Neubauer (CSU) instructed his officials to correct the pension decision. However, a withdrawal of the dubious decision was "no longer possible for legal reasons," he later said at a press conference. In return, the minister ordered that the war victims' pension should be excluded from increases until the disputed compensation for damages had been exhausted. Despite the headlines, the letters to the editor and the fierce debates, the affair surrounding the pension payments to Freisler's widow was by no means unusual.

The fact that surviving dependents of Nazi elites claimed pension rights and compensation after the war may seem grotesque, even cynical, to many, but the regulations of the Federal Pension Act also contained a bureaucratic niche for these relatives. As early as the 1950s, Lina Heydrich, the widow of the "Final Solution" mastermind SS-*Obergruppenführer* Reinhard Heydrich, the daughters of Hermann Göring and Heinrich Himmler, and the widow of the Franconian Gauleiter Julius Streicher, who had her husband reinsured for his early independent work as editor of the Nazi propaganda paper *Der Stürmer* and took out 46,000 marks against him, had already benefitted from this system. Dr Ernst Lautz, senior Reich lawyer at the People's Court and responsible for countless death sentences, received an additional payment of 125,000 marks on top of his pension after the war. The State Secretary in Hitler's Ministry of Justice, Dr Curt Rothenberger, who was sentenced to seven years in prison at Nuremberg, was paid back 190,726 marks, in addition to his substantial pension of over 2,000 marks per month.

What was new about the Freisler case, however, was that not only were the basic rights of war victims and previous "merits" asserted, but also that a Nazi criminal's working life was artificially extended until retirement age. The reasoning may have been absurd – and yet almost everything spoke for the correctness of the Munich officials' opinion. Freisler was undoubtedly one of the prominent mass murderers of the Nazi system: during the time of his presidency – from 1942 to 1945 – and partly under his personal chairmanship, the People's Court promulgated an average of ten death sentences per day.

Of course, if Freisler had fallen into the Allies' hands at the end of the war and been one of the main criminals at the Nuremberg Trials, then there might have been a chance for him to receive a fair judgement.

But even at the Nuremberg Trials, the accused were only given prison sentences, which, thanks to a generous practice of pardons, none of the convicts had to serve in full. In any case, expiatory justice towards their former colleagues could not be expected from the Federal German judiciary. By the 1950s, the Federal Court of Justice had drawn a line under the past with a dubious ruling that granted all Nazi judges a double privilege to pervert the law: a judge may only be convicted of murder or other serious crimes if he is also found guilty of bending the law. This required proof of direct intent on the part of the Nazi lawyers, which was almost impossible to obtain. The perpetrator must have deliberately or intentionally violated the legal system in force at the time. An absurd justification. Almost all judges in the Third Reich, but especially those murderers of the People's Court, acted in complete accordance with the laws of the Nazi state. In Freisler's case, proof of such an intention to bend the law would have been considerably more difficult than for any of his fellow Nazi judges, who survived the war and generally continued their judicial career in the Adenauer state.

Statistics from the Berlin judiciary on members of the People's Court who were still alive speak volumes. Among the lawyers still alive at the time of the survey in 1984 were: two district judges, one district court director, two district court councilors, four regional court directors, four higher regional court judges, six prosecutors, three chief prosecutors and even two Senate presidents. It remained the exception that one of the VGH lawyers was not taken on in the civil service after the war. So why should Freisler not have been safe from prosecution and enjoyed a second career? In this respect, the arguments made by the Munich social bureaucrats were not without a certain logic. Indeed, Freisler had a "classic" German career.

Margot Diestel, one of the few surviving victims, a woman who only survived her death sentence because the Nazi dictatorship was literally in ruins, received 920 marks for her martyrdom – a one-time compensation for her pain and suffering. The widow of the man who sentenced her to death received a lucrative pension. It is not the fact it was paid that is scandalous, rather the reasoning behind it. What is even more depressing is that Freisler – like countless of his fellow Nazi judges – would have served the Second Republic as a civil servant and continued to make a career as a "guardian of the law" or, like thousands of other Nazi death judges, would have been paid well to retire.

Perhaps he would have sat in a condominium in Garmisch-Partenkirchen or on Lake Bodensee for many years, feeling he had nothing to blame himself for. Like many of his fellow judges, such as the ex-military lawyers Schwinge and Filbinger, he would have felt himself a man of noble disposition, a jurist, who at the time had only done his patriotic duty. And anyone who sat across from this old man with the sharp rhetoric would have understood that Roland Freisler was not a demon in a red robe. No, he was just a particularly consistent enforcer of National Socialist legal concepts. A paragon of his trade – a professional killer of a murderous system.

The old Herr Freisler need not have had a guilty conscience because of his past actions. Like almost all his fellow Nazi judges, the German post-war lawyers would have taken it from him long beforehand.

THE MAN AT THE GUILLOTINE
A GERMAN EXECUTIONER'S LIFE

Johann Reichhart is a busy man. Yesterday he was in Vienna, before that Dresden and Berlin, and now he is on his way to Munich. For years he has been crossing the country by train or in his Opel Blitz. Always on business trips, on behalf of justice. His profession: executioner. Common murderers, robbers and sex criminals die under his guillotine. Now, in 1943, he often has to deal with a new type of perpetrator: *"Volksschädlinge"* (harmful organisms), *"Wehrkraftzersetzer"* (underminers of military force) and *"Kriegswirtschaftsverbrecher"* (war economy criminals).

Day after day, Nazi special courts handed down death sentences against which there were no legal remedies. And so the executioner traveled a great deal, driving from execution to execution to do his bloody work. Reichhart had a lot of practice in ending people's lives.

Four years earlier, his activities had been regulated by a circular from the Ministry of Justice on "actions in connection with death sentences". The details of an execution were meticulously listed on twenty-one type-written pages, from the announcement of the Führer's decision, the place of execution and accommodation for the executioner, to the manner of execution and what would happen afterwards to the body. Step by step. All preparations for the execution – it was said – were to be implemented as quickly and quietly as possible.

Reichhart carried out this "necessity of war" action to the full satisfaction of his employer. In the afternoon of the day before the execution at the latest, he traveled with his two assistants, moved into quarters in nearby offices with sleeping accommodation (sometimes even in an inn), then inspected the execution site and familiarized himself with the equipment. Next, he was given an order form, the wording of which he knew almost by heart:

> *The executioner. . .Reichhart. . .is commissioned to execute the person legally sentenced to death and to the permanent loss of honor rights. . .(before and after). . .to be executed via guillotine after the Führer and Reich Chancellor had decided that justice should be given free rein.*

On 22 February 1943, justice was given free rein again. Reichhart received a message saying that in a few hours, he must carry out a death sentence on three young students. Only four days earlier, on 18 February, they had been caught by the caretaker distributing leaflets against the Hitler regime in the courtyard of Munich University. He immediately informed the Gestapo, who arrested them on the same day. They were then sent swiftly to the notorious Gestapo prison in Wittelsbach Palace. The students' names were the siblings Sophie and Hans Scholl, and Christoph Probst.

The hearing at the People's Court, responsible for cases of high treason, would be presided over by Roland Freisler. Having been President only a few months, he would travel all the way from Berlin for the occasion, determined to make a public example of the three students. Freisler's debating style was feared: he yelled at the accused, humiliated them, and violated all legal principles that were still at least halfway valid. His court cases resembled Stalinist show trials. For most of the defendants who had to answer to the fanatical judge, their death sentence was already a given fact before the trial even began: "Death by guillotine!"

After a trial lasting less than two hours, Freisler's icy voice cut through the silence of the courtroom: "The defendants Sophie Scholl, Hans Scholl and Christoph Probst are sentenced to death!" Immediately afterwards, the three students were transferred to Munich's central execution prison at Stadelheim, where the executioner Johann Reichhart had already received the order for immediate execution in the usual paper form.

Reichhart and the Stadelheim magistrates knew each other well, with a close, collegiate relationship developing between them over the years. When the new "guidelines for executioners" came into force shortly after the beginning of the war, the number of execution sites was increased from eleven to fourteen and the areas of responsibility of the four executioners had been reorganized. Johann Reichhart was now a regular at Stadelheim. He was responsible for "District II", which included the prisons in Dresden, Frankfurt (Preungesheim), Munich (Stadelheim), Stuttgart and Vienna. As a native of Bavaria, Stadelheim was the most preferable of all his jobs, even calling it his "home execution site". He had carried out countless executions here, but of course, the execution of three young people was not an everyday occurrence for him, either.

When Sophie Scholl was brought in by a prison guard, she was wearing a white dress. Shortly before, her parents had managed to speak to her and her brother Hans again. A final farewell. Sophie seemed calm and was friendly towards the prison officers. Perhaps that was why the officials took the risk of letting the three death row inmates share a cigarette together before their execution.

The guillotine was in a wooden barracks in the prison yard. Reichhart's assistants grabbed the young Sophie and lay her on the bench. Seconds later, her head was separated from her body. Next, Hans lay his head on the block. Before the cold iron rushed down, he shouted: "Long live freedom!" Finally, the same sentence was carried out on Christoph Probst, a young father of three children, who was baptized before the execution.

Three young people, denounced by a caretaker for the "unlawful distribution" of a leaflet, sentenced to death by a fanatical Nazi judge, and treated indifferently by the German people.

The assistants routinely cleaned the guillotine of blood, after which the execution protocol was duly signed. The executions were – as the minutes soberly noted – carried out in the "name of the people" and "without any particular incident" in the presence of witnesses. Reichhart had fulfilled his executioner's craft properly and without any hassle. In the following months he would behead the remaining resistance fighters from the inner circle of the "White Rose" resistance group: the medical student Alexander Schmorell, his fellow student Willi Graf and the professor of psychology and musicology Kurt Huber.

Now, he could submit his invoices: he received 40 Reichsmarks for each beheading, while 30 Reichsmarks were paid to each assistant. In the case of "multiple executions" taking place on one day, an additional 30 marks for each execution was paid. A bonus of 60 marks was paid for working away from home, but Reichhart could not claim this for work carried out in Munich as it only applied when the distance between the places of residence and execution was over 300 kilometers. However, once his work had been completed, he could finally return to his house in Gleißental, near Deisendorf, which he was able to buy in the autumn of 1942. His income had risen satisfyingly within just a few years, thanks to the increasing number of death sentences he had to carry out. Indeed, in addition to his annual basic income of 3,000 Reichsmarks, in 1943 he received further special payments totaling 41,000 marks for overseeing 764 beheadings. Reichhart, who as a young man had completed an apprenticeship as a butcher, was now financially secure as a state-hired executioner. It was what he had always dreamed of.

His rise began after the end of the First World War. He had returned home from the war in 1918 without any injuries and, in those economically difficult times, had tried his hand at being an innkeeper, book salesman and dance teacher, all with little success. Only an offer from his uncle, who was also an executioner, was to bring about the turnaround.

Franz Xaver Reichhart had been appointed as an executioner towards the end of the nineteenth century. First working as an assistant, after 1894 he was an executioner with the rank of a Bavarian civil servant. When he retired at the age of 73, after more than thirty years in the role, he had beheaded fifty-eight people. Despite his bloody craft, he saw himself as a devout Christian, lighting a candle for each person he executed and having a funeral mass read, at his own expense, to save the souls of the criminals he had beheaded.

At the suggestion of the uncle, his nephew Johann, now 31 years old, took over the executioner's position. On the one hand out of commitment to his uncle, who had always stood by him when he had financial difficulties, but on the other hand because he hoped to obtain a permanent position in the Bavarian civil service during the ongoing economic crisis. There was also a certain aspect of vanity involved: now he held an office that demanded respect. He also now had the power to transport a person from life to death, later even gladly boasting to be the "fastest executioner in Germany". On 27 March 1924 he signed his employment contract with the First Public Prosecutor of the Munich I Regional Court. In cumbersome, official German, it meticulously listed what the Free State of Bavaria expected from its future executioner. Reichhart was now ready to kill people, in the name of the people.

Johann Reichhart and his assistants could now get to work. His uncle had already taught him all the necessary skills, and he himself used the time before he took up his duties to practice on the guillotine, first with dummies, later on a corpse provided by the coroner's office.

On 24 July 1924, his time had come. Reichhart was ordered to his first execution in the district court prison of the Lower Bavarian town of Landshut. Since there was only one guillotine for the entire state of Bavaria, it had to be transported from

Stadelheim Prison in Munich to various locations. This was usually done by train. Before the heavy equipment set off on its journey, it was checked point by point to ensure it was still usable. A record was made of each examination – order must always be maintained.

In the presence of a witness, the box containing the drop-sword machine was opened. The drop-sword machine and its blade accessories were in the boxes and were complete and intact. The drop-sword machine was then screwed to the block, a blade inserted, and a double test carried out by the executioner Reichhart. The test revealed a completely correct functioning of the machine. The machine was then dissembled again and locked, together with the blades. The keys were taken by First Public Prosecutor Friedrich.

Reichhart would only decide which blade to use once he was on site and had looked through the spyhole of the prison cell to get an idea of the physical constitution of the inmate. His assistants would later attest that he soon developed an unruly knack of selecting the right weapon for each case in a matter of seconds.

When several executions were scheduled for the same day, it was preferable to change the blade each time. Only years later, in the last months of war, when there were sometimes more than a dozen death sentences to be carried out in a single day, would the same blade be used for all executions.

Reichhart was now a busy man. In the first year in his role he carried out seven executions, in the following year nine. More and more often, however, and especially in 1928, death sentences were instead commuted to life imprisonment. While this shows a humanitarian attitude within the judiciary of the Weimar Republic, as a consequence it meant that his income as an executioner began to decrease. On 11 March 1929, he therefore applied to the Bavarian State Ministry of Justice for an additional salary:

The undersigned submits the humble request to the high Ministry of Justice to grant a special remuneration for the year 1928. The reasons for this are as follows: My last execution was on 20 January 1928 in Kempten. In the meantime, I often suffered the loss of income due to the frequent waiting [for the next execution]. *My earnings are so inferior that I can only eke out a living with five people, my average income is 50 to 70 marks, but I often earn nothing for the whole week.*

I would like to ask the High Ministry of Justice to pay me a special renumeration for the year 1928 for loss of earning and loss of honor.

The ministry obliged Reichhart and granted him a one-off special payment of 500 Reichsmarks for missed executions. It also granted him permission to take up a secondary employment of any kind. Naturally, the Ministry could not compensate him for his "lost honor" and despite the additional payment, Reichhart was disappointed. He even considered ending his executioner's career; the economic situation was too precarious for him and his family. At one stage he moved to The Hague in the Netherlands and established himself as a grocer, returning to his homeland every now and again for the occasional execution. Unfortunately, thanks to an indiscretion, the true identity of this German greengrocer in the Dutch province spread around and the customers stayed away. Who wanted to buy fruit and vegetables from a German executioner?

When the National Socialists came to power in Germany on 30 January 1933, Reichhart believed an improvement was in sight. Upon his return, he was told that his experience as an executioner would be needed in the new State.

As early as June 1933 he was given a new contract guaranteeing him an annual income of 3,000 Reichsmarks. The increase was helped by the fact that the justice ministries of Bavaria and Saxony had reached the agreement that Reichhart would now also carry out executions in Saxony. From then on, he traveled (always elegantly dressed in a tailcoat and a top hat) to Dresden and Weimar, where the state of Saxony provided him with their own assistants. Although he did not become a civil servant, as he had always wished, he once again had a regular income equivalent to that of a senior government official. Finally.

A few months later, his salary was increased again to 3,720 Reichsmarks. His ultimate employer was no longer the Bavarian Ministry of Justice, but, through the transfer of sovereign rights to the Reich, he now worked for the Reich Minister of Justice based in Berlin. There, too, his impeccably professional attitude was quickly appreciated. Nothing stood in the way of his career advancement: he was regarded as a loyal supporter of Hitler's party, and a man who consciously put himself at the service of the new state, one in which he would soon gain dubious fame. An adaptable, obedient executioner with the right political leanings – in short, the ideal "German" executioner.

The correct "German" method of execution, however, was a constant matter for discussion at the Ministry of Justice. A special commission was set up to answer the question of which method of beheading was the most expedient and "appropriate", and whether other methods of execution – such as shooting or the "voluntary" ingestion of poison – should be used. Finally, in the spring of 1936, the "Führer and Reich Chancellor" Adolf Hitler personally decided that the death penalty should be carried out by "the guillotine" throughout the German Reich. After a transition period until mid-1938, when executioners carried out the last executions with hand-axes, by the end of 1938 all prisons designated as central execution sites were equipped with so-called "guillotine devices".

The National Socialist court and execution machinery began to gain momentum. Each of the three executioners was assigned a clearly defined area: Reichhart was to carry out Bavarian death sentences at Stadelheim, but was instructed to bring his guillotine with him for assignments in Dresden and Weimar. Ernst Reindel was entrusted with the executions at Plötzensee (Berlin), Breslau and Königsberg, while finally, Friedrich Hehr was to carry out the death sentences in Hamburg, Hanover, Cologne and Butzbach (Hesse). After the annexation of Austria to the German Reich in 1938, the areas of operation were changed again. Reichhart, who in the meantime had become a party member (on Labor Day, 1 May 1937), would now also cover executions in Vienna.

The following applied to all executioners: not only had the type of decapitation been standardized, but the Nazi judicial office in Berlin had also specified as to when the execution must take place. Executions were previously carried out in the morning hours, but from 1942 onwards could be completed at any time of the day or night. The time from proclamation to execution was also shortened from an initial twelve hours to six hours, then finally to two or three hours, meaning the person convicted could find out in the afternoon that their execution was scheduled for later that evening.

The number of prisoners sentenced to death was soon so high that more execution sites and new executioners had to be pressed into service. Now, Johann Reichhart and his executioner colleagues carried out their bloody craft with routine precision at the twenty-two execution sites spread out across the Reich.

Individual executions were increasingly combined into multiple ones, and the execution of the death penalty soon lost its exceptionalism. As a rule, afterwards the corpses were usually sent to anatomy schools.

"Here is the place where death is happy to serve life," are words written above the main entrance of the Anatomical Institute of Berlin University Hospital, the Charité. It was customary at all times to make the corpses of executed victims available for the training of young medical professionals. There was a constant need for the disposal of the corpses, and so some institutes now saw themselves at a disadvantage when it came to allocating the bodies, especially since a large number of anatomical institutes only had a limited number of execution sites nearby. As early as 1937, one or more institutes were assigned to each of the central execution sites by a new regulation for the "allocation and distribution of the bodies of the executed", yet time and again there were lawsuits and complaints about the surrender of the corpses, even resulting in genuine arguments over their distribution.

In addition to this, the corpses of those who had been executed could be handed over to their relatives on request, which the anatomy professors considered a "sensitive" disruption to their research. In April 1939, the universities of Cologne and Greifswald complained to the State Secretary responsible in the Reich Ministry of Justice, saying "it should be legally pointed out that. . . 1. an autopsy of executed persons is generally permitted according to the usual rules and that. . . 2. the provision for the extradition of the corpse to the relatives is transferred from being mandatory to optional." In this case, it would have been much easier for the prison administration to collect "the appropriate material".

In 1943 a binding decree was finally issued for the correct procedure in the event of death in prisons, albeit with a number of special regulations. The surrender of the corpse of someone executed for high treason, treason, or political reasons was now only possible with the consent of the Gestapo, the Secret State Police – as if the executed person could betray secrets beyond death. Overall, the situation of procuring corpses for National Socialist research and teaching at medical universities changed to the extent that the Nazi judiciary issued terror verdicts and sentenced people to death on a daily basis. An employee at the biological-anatomical institute of the University of Berlin, not far from the Plötzensee Prison execution site, later described the situation:

There were corpses. Most were predominantly of young, healthy men. The majority also had something else in common: they lacked a head. The neck was neatly severed, just above shoulder height.

His boss, Institute Director Professor Stieve, was concerned about the smooth delivery of the corpses of those who had been executed, particularly in light of the increasing number of nocturnal air raids. The following is recorded from a conversation with representatives of the enforcement authorities:

We would like to see the execution of death sentences at Berlin-Plötzensee postponed to 8 pm due to the disturbances that air raids can cause at night. Professor Stieve agreed and explained that the cadavers could then be picked up the same evening, although the cadaver requirements for the upcoming semester were already covered. However, a later point in time would not be acceptable for the Institute of Anatomy, because otherwise the processing of the corpses for research purposes would extend too late into the night, meaning the doctors involved could no longer go home via public transport.

A document of banality and barbarism in barbaric times, when a bus timetable can dictate the time of an execution.

When the execution site at Berlin's Plötzensee Prison was significantly damaged during a heavy air raid on the night of 3-4 September 1943, Nazi bureaucrats immediately developed measures to ensure that the execution of death sentences did not come to a standstill.

At the time, more than 300 convicts were in their cells awaiting execution. Because the bureaucrats would not tolerate any delays, the nearby execution site at Brandenburg-Görden was given responsibility until the guillotine was restored, and so those prisoners sentenced to death were transferred there immediately. Consideration also had to be given to those convicts shot at Wehrmacht shooting stations, which is what happened in individual cases. The incumbent Reich Minister of Justice, Thierack, even expressed the idea of administering poison or gas, although this would have been extremely difficult to put into practice. In addition, his ministry decided to simplify the clemency procedure even further, with scrutiny of the petitions now to be carried out even faster so as to speed up the execution of the death sentences.

Accelerated State executions could now continue, if not with the guillotine, then with the rope. A few days after the earlier air raids, on 7 September, an initial order for the execution of 186 convicts was issued. The first executions began at 7:30 pm. Eight convicts were tied together in a row and led across the prison courtyards to the execution room, where they were hanged by the executioner Röttger and his assistants every twenty minutes.

Wilhelm Röttger, a trained horse butcher and haulier from Moabit, in Berlin, was hired to help support the three executioners. In total, he carried out by far the most death sentences of all the executioners of the Third Reich. He was paid a fixed sum of 3,000 Reichsmarks and an additional 30 marks "per head", so he knew his overall income could increase considerably the more work he took on.

Since he could not hang all eight men at the same time, he had the other seven wait at the entrance when the executions began, and then ordered them brought in, one after another. After his assistants had lifted them up, Röttger stood on a step platform and put the noose around the condemned man's neck himself. Once the noose had been attached to a hook, the assistants released the body. Loss of consciousness was instant.

In the execution mania, six people who had not been on the list submitted by the Reich Ministry of Justice were also hanged. But what value is a human life, whether previously sentenced to death for something trivial or accidentally imprisoned on one of the death rows? In September 1943 alone, Röttger executed a total of 324 people in Plötzensee and Brandenburg-Görden in order to "quickly reduce the number of people sentenced to death", as instructed. His bonus of 30 Reichsmarks per head was immediately transferred to him by Nazi officials.

By late 1943, when the euphoria of war had waned, resistance against the Nazi regime intensified. After the assassination attempt on Hitler on 20 July 1944, death sentences were imposed more and more frequently by special courts, which the executioners struggled to cope with. This led to the use of so-called "Party executioners", who were not only means of "reinforcement", but also acted as competition for the traditional executioners.

In 1937, three State-appointed men carried out the executioner's trade. Six years later, the list of executioners appointed by the Reich Ministry of Justice included ten names: Gottlob Bordt, Friedrich Hehr, Karl Henschke, August Köster, Johann Mühl, Ernst Reindel, Wilhelm Röttger, Alois Weiss, Fritz Witzka, and, finally, Johann Reichhart. Alfred Roselieb was added to the list in 1944.

On 17 January 1945, new guidelines were once again announced. Paragraph six was extended by one point: "The German salute is to be avoided at the place of execution." In addition, scheduling issues can now be resolved by either shooting or hanging the accused. Death by shooting was now possible "if execution by beheading causes difficulties or delays".

In early 1945 the special courts in Germany continued to pass death sentences, while the executioners and their assistants carried them out. Until the bitter end. As the country sank into ash and rubble, the downfall of the "Thousand Year Reich" was imminent, but the Nazi executioners carried on their bloody work, as instructed.

In the end they carried out more than 16,000 death sentences, of which 11,881 were completed by the three executioners Johann Reichhart, Wilhelm Röttger and Ernst Reindel. It was Reindel who, as the merciless "Butcher of Berlin", on Hitler's orders hanged the co-conspirators of 20 July Plot from meat hooks. At Hitler's request, his cruel actions were filmed by a camera team commissioned by of Reich Film Director Hans Hinkel.

On 16 April 1945, even as Berlin was already being heavily fought over, executions were still taking place at Plötzensee. Röttger, Reindel, Reinhart and their colleagues were killing to the end – their executioner work had by now become a barbaric routine.

Did they have any scruples? Any morals? Any pity for what they were doing? Surely everyone was only carrying out their national "duty", whether at the guillotine, in the courtroom or in the Ministry of Justice: executioners, justice secretaries, prosecutors, judges, prison guards, medical professors, doctors, cameramen – they were all carrying out their duties fanatically and conscientiously for the Führer, the people and the Fatherland. Until the last day, until the last hour, until the end of the war. Until the downfall.

Then the war was over. Lost, said the Germans. The madness had ended and with it the barbarism. Now the collective cleansing began. No one wanted to be a perpetrator, a follower, a visionary anymore. And Johann Reichhart? Did he now blame himself for what he had done? Can something be wrong now, he wondered, what had been right just a few weeks ago? Had he not always maintained law and order? Had he not exercised his craft to the best of his ability, just as the gentlemen at the Ministry of Justice had stipulated and ordered in their guidelines? Had he not, as was his duty and role as an executioner, duly carried out all the sentences the prosecutors had demanded and the judges had pronounced? Was he not reliable, law-abiding, consistent – just as he had been instructed to be in his employment contract?

American forces liberated Munich on 30 April 1945, and the victors passed judgement on the vanquished. Now more death sentences were to be enforced. In mid-May, US soldiers drove to Johann Reichhart's house in Gleißental, where he had withdrawn to for fear of arrest. The Americans had received information that the "Damned Nazi Murderer" was staying there, so they picked him up, tied his hands and drove him in a Jeep to Stadelheim Prison, in Munich. This was where he had carried out many of his more than 1,200 death sentences before the end of the war, including those of numerous, innocent resistance fighters such as the Scholl siblings. Should he, who had beheaded so many people with the guillotine, now also be executed as a war criminal?

The executioner's imprisonment was short-lived. After just one week, the prison gates were opened for him. American officers took him to the prison at the nearby Landsberg am Lech, where Adolf Hitler had once been imprisoned after his attempted putsch, and now where Nazi war criminals filled the cells. Reichhart suspected what the Americans wanted from him: they needed him for the same role the state of Bavaria had needed him for during the Weimar Republic and the previous years under the National Socialists. And so, Johann Reichhart found himself an executioner once again, just a few weeks after the end of the war, but this time for the American military government.

Two new gallows were built in the Landsberg prison yard. Reichhart knew what to do. In 1942 he had constructed a gallows himself based on the English model, but this had been rejected by the Reich Ministry of Justice because the Nazi lawyers had preferred the more agonizing variant of strangulation for hanging delinquents, which was reintroduced that same year as a particularly dishonorable punishment alongside the guillotine. Two assistants lifted the person to be executed up, while at the same time the executioner placed a rope around their neck. On command, the assistants pushed the shoulders of the bound body towards the floor. Death occurred after a few seconds. Reichhart and his men accomplished this form of killing in Landsberg with quick precision.

In return for his expertise, Reichhart enjoyed certain privileges. When death sentences were to be carried out, he was collected from his home in Gleißental by a military Jeep and chauffeured to Landsberg Prison. Instead of money he received canned food, alcohol and cigarettes: an attractive form of currency in the post-war period. Reichhart tied the noose 165 times to bring Nazi Party celebrities, concentration camp henchmen and SS bigwigs to their deaths. The American military judiciary was so convinced of its executioner's services that it even considered appointing him as the executioner for those Nazi greats who were condemned to death at the Nuremberg Trials. However, the military government changed its mind, and Reichhart's role was reduced to instructing US Sergeant Hazel Woods in the "art of hanging from the gallows". On 16 October 1946, it was Woods who finally put the noose around the necks of the death row inmates, including Frank, Frick, Jodl, Kaltenbrunner, Keitel, Ribbentrop, Rosenberg and Streicher.

A few months earlier, in August 1945, the Munich city administration had received an advertisement addressed to the then Lord Mayor Karl Scharnagl, in which, with reference to Reichhart's privileged living arrangements, a prosecution for his activities during the Nazi regime and his expropriation were demanded. The complaint was forwarded to the relevant public prosecutor's office, although it showed little interest in taking criminal action against the former Nazi executioner. As long as he was still providing his services to the American military government, they were obviously unwilling to take action. After all, Reichhart was still a Bavarian civil servant. On 6 April 1946, and later on 7 February 1947, the Bavarian State Ministry of Justice concluded a new employment contract with him, which was now also the basis for his work as an executioner for the US military government.

But Reichhart's situation became precarious. A few months later, in May 1947, the military police took Reichhart from his apartment to an internment camp, albeit a very special camp, of course, at Moosburg an der Isar. The camp was reserved for "special officials of the NSDAP" and for senior SA and SS members. Here the former executioner met Hitler's former Vice Chancellor Franz von Papen, *Feldmarschall* Sperrle, as well as Emmy Göring, the wife of *Reichsmarschall* Hermann Göring. It was most likely Emmy who had smuggled the cyanide capsule into her husband's prison cell, who had otherwise been sentenced to death by hanging.

So, Reichhart was in good company, but the prominent inmates avoided him when they found out who he was. In December 1948, when he had to answer to a Munich tribunal for his work as a Nazi executioner, he used his closing remarks to express his bitter disappointment at how the judiciary, in particular, had treated him:

I have carried out death sentences in the firm conviction that I serve the State with my work and that I comply with the legitimate laws. Only now have I become fully aware of how much I was exploited, even abused, by the State and its superiors in my blind faith and obedience. I beheaded and hanged murderers, violent criminals, traitors and those harmful to others because I did not doubt the legality of the death sentences. However, I will do everything I can to ensure that I was the last Reichhart to push himself into the office of messenger. In the future, may the judges carry out the death sentences themselves.

In total, Reichhart carried out 3,126 death sentences – 250 of them against women – from 1924 to 1945. He executed murderers and violent criminals, but also resistance fighters and alleged opponents of the Nazi regime. On the orders of the American military powers, he hanged a further 156 people. His 23-year career as an executioner made him wealthy; in 1943 alone he earned the enormous sum of 41,748 Reichsmarks. In the end, however, he was an isolated old man who received a modest disability and military pension of just 220 marks per month. He ran a dog breeding center in Deisendorf, near Munich, and only came into the public eye again when it was revealed that he had been made an honorary member of the *"Verein zur Wiederein einführung der Todesstrafe"* (Association for the Reintroduction of the Death Penalty).

In 1974, shortly before his seventy-ninth birthday, Johann Reichhart died in a hospital near Munich.

THE FORGOTTEN HEROES
RESISTANCE FIGHTERS GEORG ELSER AND MAURICE BAVAUD

The bomb exploded at 9:20 pm on the evening of 8 November 1939. Beams cracked, walls burst, part of the ceiling collapsed. There were screams of horror and panic. Seven people died under the rubble; an eighth would not survive their injuries. More than sixty people were injured, some seriously. Hitler, the target of the bomb, survived. Thirteen minutes before detonation, he had finished his speech in the hall of the *Bürgerbräukeller* in Munich, which had been filled with over 3,000 "old guard". As his Nazi Party comrades had continued to shout "Heil", their leader had climbed down from the lectern and – quite contrary to his usual habit – had left the hall with his entourage to catch a special train to Berlin that evening. Had he still been standing at his lectern, he would not have survived the attack. When news of the bombing reached him on the train, he said to his companions: "My leaving the *Bürgerbräukeller* earlier than usual is proof to me that Providence wants me to reach my goal."

The nation-wide hunt for the assassin came to a rapid conclusion. While Hitler was still giving his abridged speech, a slim man was arrested near Konstanz while trying to cross the border into Switzerland illegally. His name: Georg Elser, 36 years old, a journeyman carpenter from the Ostalb. The customs officers found the following incriminating objects on him: a postcard of the Munich *Bürgerbräukeller*, wires and cartridges, and a notebook containing the addresses of explosives manufacturers. The small, slender man remained silent. The officers took Elser to the Gestapo. The interrogations became tougher but remained unsuccessful. The next morning, he was taken to Munich where a special investigation was taking place. This time the interrogations did not stop at threats. There were beatings, too. For four days. Yet still without a result. On the fifth day, Elser confessed. He asked his tormentors: "What do you get for doing something like that?"

But who was this inconspicuous craftsman? A would-be martyr? In reality, Georg Elser was anything but an idealistic crank. The people of Königsbronn knew him as a reserved individual who led an ordinary life. He was not a party member; politics did not interest him. However, he suffered from what was happening around him, even while his compatriots cheered.

The area around Württemberg is a stronghold of Pietism, whose people have a strong sense of justice. Someone like Elser, a pedantic, meticulous craftsman, would always prefer to be his own master, lacking any prerequisite for adapting to the national spirit of optimism. His sense of justice and deep-rooted self-righteous character gave him the energy to spend more than a year, from autumn 1938 onwards, planning and preparing the assassination with his usual conscientiousness and perseverance. This was all preceded by a difficult question of conscience: violence is profoundly alien to the Pietist, his religiosity forbidding him from murdering tyrants. Nevertheless, Elser decided to carry out the attack. He saw no other way of stopping the impending disaster. He was a man of stubbornness and courage in an ocean of opportunism.

He inspected the *Bürgerbräukeller* in Munich, made drawings, procured explosives. On the night of 5 August 1939, he began to work on the pillar intended to conceal his bomb. Under the glow of his flashlight, he broke away sections of the masonry piece by piece, later throwing the rubble into the Isar. He worked for thirty-five nights, but by 6 November, it was ready. A day later, he returned again to ensure the built-in mechanisms were working before leaving for Konstanz.

Three weeks later, after his arrest at the Swiss border, his confession in Munich and further interrogations at the Berlin Reich Security Main Office, Elser was taken from prison to Sachsenhausen concentration camp, 80 kilometers away. The Nazis' plan was to put him in a show trial after the end of the war and use him as a witness against the British secret service. He would be portrayed as a tool used by British spies who wanted to kill Hitler. As an important prisoner for Nazi propaganda, he enjoyed preferential treatment, living in a two-man cell and working in a small carpentry shop. At all other times he was completely isolated. No letters reached him, while his own letters remained unanswered.

Five years later, Germany was staring at defeat in the war. The Nazis' star witness, Georg Elser, was no longer needed, so at the end of 1944 he was taken to Dachau. On 5 April 1945, Himmler sent an express letter to the camp commandant. It stated succinctly: "The question of our prisoner in special protective custody, Elser, has again been discussed at the highest level. The following directions have been issued: Elser will allegedly suffer fatal injuries in one of the next Terror Attacks on Munich or the surroundings of Dachau. To this end, I would ask that Elser be liquidated as discretely as possible." That is exactly how it was done. On 9 April, Elser was shot from behind by concentration camp guards.

Until a few years ago, Georg Elser had led a shadowy existence in the gallery of German resistance fighters. Unlike Count von Stauffenberg, four years his senior, he was not suited for the role of the state-glorified hero. He was not the educated officer who had initially trusted and committed himself to the promises of the Nazi regime, only later to turn against it and take decisive action. Instead, we have the demure, reserved journeyman carpenter Elser, with only a primary school diploma who, in 1939, when Stauffenberg and millions of other Germans were still cheering for the Führer, had already recognized the murderous character of the regime and made the decision to carry out the assassination.

Stauffenberg saw himself first as a soldier, following in the centuries-old tradition of his family. Although he would later lose all enthusiasm for National Socialism, he had nothing but contempt for parliamentary democracy throughout his life. His understanding of morality was a complex conglomeration of Catholic doctrine, an aristocratic code of honor, the ethos of ancient Greece and German Romantic poetry. His bold decision to kill Hitler with a bomb was an expression of military rather than moral considerations. The coincidence by which Hitler escaped with his life, the hopeless situation of the co-conspirators, the hasty execution of Stauffenberg, it was all a deep tragedy. Count von Stauffenberg was a courageous patriot, but also a strict anti-democrat.

There is no question that Georg Elser was a challenge, not only for his home region, but also for the German public. He had made it clear that a simple man of the people could pull himself together to carry out a globally historical action. He gave the lie to all those who continued to convince themselves that they could have done nothing to counteract the terror of the Nazi state. His actions shamed many Germans.

Elser was always a loner. Although he felt connected to the workers' movement, he was close to the Communist Party without ever being a member. However, he did not allow himself to be stylized as a solid, even exemplary comrade. Ideological questions had little interest for him. What does public appreciation for such a man look like? How is he remembered?

Societies do not remember the past purely in relation to what is better for them. Remembrance needs a group that supports it: aristocratic, military, social-democratic, communist or ecclesiastical resistance is remembered by their respective groups. So where does Elser fit in?

Georg Elser fared like many other men and women of the resistance in that politically, post-war Germany was more concerned with the reintegration of Nazi perpetrators than the rehabilitation of its victims. Worse still, lawyers who had faithfully served the Nazi regime were once again in court and passing judgements.

An example here is the reparation proceeding in the Maurice Bavaud case, which was heard at the Berlin district court in 1955. Indeed, the story of the young man from Switzerland has numerous parallels to that of Georg Elser. In October 1938, 22-year-old Maurice bought a pistol and traveled to Germany to kill Hitler. From Berlin he traveled to Munich, where he had to abandon his plan to shoot Hitler during the SA's memorial march to the *Felderrnhalle* because his line of sight was not good enough. Bavaud was later caught on the Munich–Paris train without a ticket, became involved in an altercation, and was finally handed over to the Gestapo, who interrogated him and managed to extract a confession. Sentenced to death by the People's Court, he was executed by guillotine at Plötzensee Prison, Berlin, in May 1941.

Not only is Bavaud not remembered by posterity, he was also condemned again ten years after the end of the war by the country's judiciary, which had previously guided him from his young life to his death. Bavaud's family had requested a retrial against the Federal Republic of Germany. They were also seeking a compensation payment for 40,000 francs, which, of course, could only be paid as "damages" if Maurice was subsequently acquitted by a German court. But Hitler's assassin, who had already been executed in 1941, was sentenced a second time: this time to five years in prison. No money was paid and no other decision possible because, according to the court, "Hitler's life was to be recognized in the same way as any other protected legal interest within the meaning of paragraph 211 of the Criminal Code. The application for annulment of the death sentence of the People's Court of 18 December 1939 is rejected."

Bavaud's civil rights had been revoked for life by the People's Court, despite his death sentence. Now, the post-war lawyers had pardoned him to five years' deprivation of these rights. How the dead man was to serve five years in prison was not explained in detail. Only in a third trial – in 1956 – was the death sentence from 1939 finally lifted and imprisonment no longer imposed. Finally, the Federal Republic of Germany transferred 40,000 Swiss francs to the Bavaud family, who had to confirm that "the affair was unquestionably settled".

Georg Elser and Maurice Bavaud: two Hitler assassins who dared to do "it" earlier than any other, without any support from a resistance group. They paid for it with their lives.

For a long time, neither of them found their way into the history of the resistance against Hitler, not just because historians could not agree on their motives for their actions. Elser's attempt was the subject of great dispute in Munich for forty years before the city's government decided to honor him. Today, more than seventy years after his attempted assassination, Georg Elser has finally been rehabilitated: more than fifty streets and squares and three schools throughout Germany are now named after him, and in 2003, the Post Office even issued a special Georg Elser stamp. In 2010 the small Swabian town where he was born commemorated him with a 2.10-meter-high steel monument, located right next to the train station. In Berlin's government district there is a bust of Elser on the banks of the Spree in the "Street of Remembrance", next to Thomas Mann, Edith Stein and Walter Rathenau, the murdered Foreign Minister of the Weimar Republic. Since November 2011 there has been a 17-meter-high sculpture in the middle of the old government quarter on Wilhelmsstraße; a steel band with a string of lights outlining Elser's profile. The German playwright Rolf Hochhith, who unveiled the memorial, wanted the silhouette to rise "above the place of the perpetrators" near Adolf Hitler's former bunker. The fleeting passer-by, who may not recognize Elser, can find out via a small information board who is honored there. The "memorial", with the curved neon tubes, is a little like an advertisement; the individual only becomes visible at second glance. Even now, Georg Elser, the withdrawn man, the solitaire, who only followed his sense of justice, does not push himself into the foreground.

In the meantime, there has also been also audible criticism of the "creepy culture of remembrance of Georg Elser". Critics state that Elser offers himself as a role model because he is "far easier to use for self-assurance" than, for example, the elitist officer Stauffenberg, a conservative conspirator like Carl Friedrich Goerdeler, or even members of communist resistance cells such as the "Red Orchestra". He is therefore suitable as an optimal target for all subsequent opposition to National Socialism and is ideally suited as a role model for all "contemporary good people". As if the mere acknowledgement of Elser and his actions alone was some form of courageous attitude to have.

The historian Angelika Nußberger has pointed out in a worthy essay the instrumentalization of the fates of those people who stood out from the crowd in a certain historical context, and how legal and moral evaluations and judgements change in retrospect. Assassins and traitors to the Fatherland later become heroes.

This also applies to German resistance fighters. The fact that, from today's point of view, the Nazi era was a barbaric time in terms of wars of aggression, racial ideology and the Holocaust makes it somewhat easy to identify all opponents of the system as upstanding and honest, as courageous people. They are undeniably heroes. Anyone who pays respect to those who fought against the unlawful National Socialist state, for whatever reason, is on the side of democracy and the rule of law. Anyone who admires them will not be met with much opposition. According to Nußberger, they are "comfortable" heroes. Today, Georg Elser is a "comfortable hero".

This does not change anything about his beliefs. Ever since the former Federal Chancellor Helmut Kohl publicly paid tribute to Elser, the question "Who does Elser belong to?" has become obsolete. The great historian Joseph Peter Stern once called Elser a "man without ideology". There is nothing to add to this. It also applies to Maurice Bavaud.

THE FÜHRER LIVES
OR: HITLER AS A MEDIA POP STAR

The Führer is back. *"Er ist wieder da"* (Look Who's Back) was the name of the enormously successful film based on the Hitler novel by Timur Vermes, which had already stormed the bestseller charts. In the film, the director lets his main actor travel through the republic in a Nazi uniform – and everyone is in good spirits. The "Führer" is enthusiastically applauded everywhere, selfies are taken. People want to be close to him. The uniform has an effect from Sylt to Bavaria. So, Hitler is back. But had he actually gone? Whatever the case, the fascination for him, it seems, is undiminished.

Hardly any historical figure can move the German people more. He is a pop star, a media and entertainment industry "sensation". His potential to excite and outrage is unsurpassed by any other historical horror figure. A magazine that puts Hitler on the cover will always sell well.

When Dani Levy's film *"Mein Führer – Die wirklich wahrste Wahrheit über Adolf Hitler"* (My Führer: The Really Truest Truth about Adolf Hitler) was released in cinemas in 2007, the excitement in the arts pages was still great: "Are you allowed to do that?" nervous journalists asked, "Laugh at Hitler?" As if Mel Brooks' "Springtime for Hitler" had never existed. Meanwhile, "The Führer" is a global media star. Indeed, Adolf Hitler has even made several appearances in the cult animated series "The Simpsons".

There is no doubt that people are now more at ease when dealing with Hitler and National Socialism. Not because the object has lost its terror, but because the terror has detached itself from the object. Whether as a film, book, or parody, it now seems as if Hitler is closer to the German people than ever, almost eighty years after the end of the war.

Guido Knopp's colorful TV documentary reports ("Hitler's Helpers", "Hitler's Women" and others) are still ratings earners even after their fifth showing. BBC series about Hitler's Nazi Germany can be seen by viewers in Phoenix in endless loops. "Documentary" TV films thrive on fictionalization, which is unstoppable if only because the last eyewitnesses are dying out.

What actually happened gives way to a historical myth that knows no contradictions. The people, the propaganda, the crimes of the National Socialists, the real horrors turn into shuddering fascination. In this way, Nazi Germany is being obscured and transferred to the present day in a more marketable way. The Nazi era has degenerated into a code of evil that can be replaced at will, with a disastrous side effect: trivialization. And this trivialization needs a face: Hitler. He has mutated into a pop-culture icon of evil.

The trivializing arbitrariness stands in stark contrast to the delusions of persecution and criminalization in the fight against any Nazi legacy. The swastika, SS runes and the *Reichskriegsflagge* (Reich war flag) are forbidden. Anyone who displays them publicly risks being taken to court. Hitler's collected propaganda prose *Mein Kampf* was out of print for decades, nor was it allowed to be sold [in Germany]. According to the legislator, the symbols and writings it contained still posed a threat. It was not until 2016 that the work – edited and commented on by historians of the Munich Institute of Contemporary History – was able to appear legally once again.

A judicial farce from Swabia shows where the attempts to exorcise Nazi symbols can lead. For almost two years, police officers, prosecutors and judges dealt with the question of whether a crossed-out swastika violated the ban on Nazi symbols. Apartments were searched, stickers and banners confiscated, fines imposed. Then the Federal Court of Justice ruled that demonstrators may use alienated Nazi symbols, NPD opponents could figuratively kick swastikas into the bin, punks could symbolically crush them with their boots or smash them with a hammer. Politicians were also allowed to integrate swastikas into red no-parking signs and to pin them to their lapels like a badge.

Unlike the Regional Court of Stuttgart, the Third Criminal Senate of the Federal Court of Justice recognized no criminal offence in this, and therefore also acquitted a mail order company of the charge of "using symbols of unconstitutional organizations". The Federal Supreme Court justified its ruling by saying that if the symbols expressed opposition to National Socialism "in an obvious and unambiguous manner", then their use should not be criminalized.

On the one hand we have the cult of Hitler the person, on the other the rigorous legal persecution and social ostracism of displaying any form of Nazi memorabilia and other Nazi legacies. A socio-psychological dichotomy, or a realpolitik grotesque?

The fact is that Hitler comparisons are still contaminated (although as a targeted breach of taboo they can be useful marketing tools, see Eva Herman and Thilo Sarrazin), but they are no longer the great border crossings that they were for so many years.

Hitler serves as a template for the supposedly dark characteristics of his personality, reduced to "evil". This evil is fascinating and menacing at the same time. We want nothing to do with him and yet cannot turn away from him. We want it out of our world and yet we need its presence.

It fits into the drama that the copyright for *Mein Kampf* expired just in time for the New Year's Eve celebrations on 31 December 2015. Although Hitler's text could always be found on the Internet, since the beginning of 2016 anyone can now do what they want with the diatribe. The entire text entered the public domain seventy years after the author's death. First published as a popular edition in 1930, it had sold over 12 million copies before being banned by the Allies in 1945. Since then, it had only been available in printed form in antiquarian bookshops. After the copyright expired, the controversial work was now back on sale.

Now it was available as a "critical edition": 1,948 pages plus 3,700 footnotes, edited and commented on by historians of the Munich Institute of Contemporary History. The historians compared 38 out of 1,122 editions, each correction being recorded and noted. Every lie and half-lie exposed. The man from Braunau am Inn had deliberately distorted many things, while his research was even sloppier. The number of factual errors alone is immense. It is to the historians' credit that they were able to "purify" the pompous and laborious "Hitler sound" of every form of ideological poison. In fact, the commentary now makes several passages of the book understandable for many readers.

The publication turned into an event. The new edition made it onto Korean breakfast television, the BBC and Al Jazeera. Italy's *La Stampa* reported on it, as did Spain's *El Pais* and the *New York Times*. All of Germany's leading media printed major magazines, while ARD and ZDF produced documentaries. The Munich historians had probably never received so much public attention.

More than 25,000 copies – for a lofty 59 Euros – have been sold so far. And if this historical edition is too extensive for your tastes, there are numerous other new releases that deal with the dubious career of the German bestseller in a less voluminous, but nevertheless profound and serious way.

The sorry story of anti-Semitism, hatred and megalomania has been told and documented. From its genesis in the early 1920s to the banning of debates today, writers have dispelled the well-known myths and exposed Hitler as a falsifier of his own biography. A meritorious and successful attempt at a necessary disenchantment.

Is there an end to Hitler? The Führer's afterlife continues in new books, films and research. His presence not only delights history-obsessed dull nostalgiacs, but the pictures drawn from it also offer many Germans – whether young or old – a welcome opportunity to reconstruct, gloss over and forget the country's Nazi past.

Hitler alone is said to have been responsible for the destruction of the German people and their millions of crimes. History, of course, does not want to go away just because it has been and gone.

NOTES AND REFERENCES

The opening quote is by Raul Hilberg (1926-2007), who shaped the historiography of the Holocaust like no other historian. His comprehensive book *Die Vernichtung der europäischen Juden: Die Gesamtgeschichte des Holocaust* (Berlin, 1982), in which the quotation can be found on p.685, was first published in the USA in 1961 and has been repeatedly revised and updated since then. It remains the authoritative study on the Holocaust to this day.

Most recently, a collection of essays and memoirs by Hilberg from the years 1965 to 2007, edited by his longtime editor Walter H. Pehle and René Schlott, was published under the title *Anatomie des Holocaust* (Frankfurt am Main, 2016).

The Past in the Present
or: Mr Hanning on trial

On the trial of SS man Reinhold Hanning, Anna Pritzkau's article *"Lage der Nation"* on FAZ.net, 18 April 2016, is well worth reading, so too the contributions about the trial of SS man Oskar Gröning: Nora Bossong's *"Das letzte Gefecht"* in *DIE ZEIT*, 16 July 2015, p.30; Hans Holzhaider's *"Der letzte Angeklagte von Auschwitz"* in *Süddeutsche Zeitung*, 11/12 July 2015, pp.11-13; and Alexander Hanecke's *"Der lange Arm der Tat"* in *Frankfurter Allgemeine Sonntagszeitung*, 31 May 2015, p.51.

On dealing with the Nazi past: Norbert Frei's *1945 und wir: Das Dritte Reich im Bewusstsein der Deutschen* (Munich, 2005), likewise the same, *Hitlers Eliten nach 1945* (Munich, 2003). The book names numerous lawyers, doctors, entrepreneurs, journalists and officers who served the Nazi regime in important positions and were later able to continue their careers in the Federal Republic of Germany, including, among others, Hermann Josef Abs, Hans Filbinger, Reinhard Gehlen, Hans Globke, Werner Höfer, Erich Manstein and Josef Neckermann. They illustrate the extent to which the emerging democracy was shaped by men with a past. A lesson in political behavior between punishment and reintegration, control and infiltration, reform and restoration.

Ernst Klee recorded the most important people in the Third Reich from the judiciary, Church, welfare institutions, culture, business, journalism, science, medicine, police and the armed forces, as well as key figures from the NSDAP, SA and SS. With its 4,300 articles, the unrivalled lexicon of persons also provides detailed information about their careers after 1945. Cf. Ernst Klee, *Das Personenlexikon zum Dritten Reich: Wer was vor und nach 1945 war* (Frankfurt am Main, 2015).

In his book *Die kalte Amnestie: NS-Täter in der Bundesrepublik* (Frankfurt am Main, 1988), Jörg Friedrich also analyses and documents the targeted integration of the Nazi perpetrator community into post-war society.

In her study, *"Ich fühl' mich nicht als Mörder!": Die Integration von NS-Tätern in die Nachkriegsgesellschaft* (Darmstadt, 2011), Christina Ullrich describes the integration of SS leaders into post-war society and the way in which they shaped their new careers using nineteen exemplary biographies.

The inglorious past of the Federal Foreign Office during the Nazi era and after 1945 was reviewed by an independent group of historians in 2005, commissioned by the Green Party's Foreign Minister Joschka Fischer. The thorough and extensive investigation also dispelled the legend that the Nazi Foreign Ministry was a haven of resistance and that the employees either knew nothing about the Holocaust or sabotaged it to the best of their ability. Rather, it was true that the office, which was dominated by German nationalist nobles, had defended and deflected the anti-Semitic policies of the Nazis from 1933 onwards. The employees joined the party in droves "like everyone else", and that the "Final Solution to the Jewish Question" was not only known in the Foreign Office, but its employees often played an active, criminal role in it.

The study also showed how the diplomatic cliques succeeded in issuing each other "*Persilscheine*" ("clean bills") after 1945. Numerous leading employees very quickly regained managerial positions at the Foreign Ministry in Bonn. It is astonishing to realize that even under Willy Brandt's leadership, little changed in this fundamental practice. The office was in no position to purge itself, nor was there the necessary political pressure to do so. If occasionally incriminated persons had to be sent into retirement, then this was usually due to the scandalization of certain cases by attentive journalists.

The study was published in book form under the title *Das Amt und die Vergangenheit: Deutsche Diplomaten im Dritten Reich und in der Bundesrepublik* (Munich, 2010), and was written and edited by the authors Eckhart Conze (Marburg), Norbert Frei (Jena), Peter Hayes (Evanstown/Illinois) and Moshe Zimmermann (Jerusalem). It is now regarded as a standard work.

The continuity of personnel in the judiciary, particularly judges and public prosecutors, is explained in the appendix of my book *Der Hinrichter: Roland Freisler – Mörder im Dienste Hitlers* (Frankfurt am Main, 2014) and is comprehensively documented.

The exception: Fritz Bauer. He forced the German people to look by pushing through the Frankfurt Auschwitz trial in the midst of a judiciary in the young Federal Republic that was still characterized by Nazi cliques. He cooperated with the Israeli secret service to bring Adolf Eichmann to justice. Only recently – not least through the film "*Der Staat gegen Fritz Bauer*"

(2015), directed by Lars Kraume – has he received belated and broad recognition.

Also worth reading is Ronen Steinke's *Fritz Bauer order Auschwitz vor Gericht* (Munich and Zürich, 2013), as well as Heribert Prantl's *"Ein Erschütterer"* in *Süddeutsche Zeitung*, 24/25 October 2015, p.55 and Erardo Christoforo Rautenberg's, *"Zu Haus unter Feinden"* in *DIE ZEIT*, 13 November 2014, p.17.

Ralph Giordano impressively describes the institutional, political and social delays and failures in post-war Germany in *Die zweite Schuld oder Von der Last Deutscher zu sein* (Hamburg, 1987).

On the collective guilt of the war and post-war generation, its confrontation with National Socialism and its consequences, the special role of the judiciary and the possibilities of forgiveness and reconciliation, see Bernhard Schlink's *Vergangenheitsschuld – Beiträge zu einem deutschen Thema* (Zürich, 2007).

On the socio-psychological foundations of collective repression, see also Alexander and Margaret Mitscherlich, *Die Unfähigkeiten zu trauern* (Munich, 1967). The quotation from Hans Globke can be found on pp.313-14.

The attempts to "liberate" the German people from their gloomy past not only boomed in the Adenauer Republic, but also continue to this day, as Hannes Heer shows in *"Hitler war's"* – *Die Befreiung der Deutschen von ihrer Vergangenheit* (Berlin, 2005).

Why millions of Germans voted for Hitler and why the National Socialists as a party were able to win over all sections of the population is answered knowledgeably by Peter Fritzsche in *Wie aus Deutschen Nazis wurden* (Zurich, 1999).

An outstanding, textbook example of a career as a Nazi criminal in post-war Germany can be found in the person of Hans Globke, formerly co-author of the Nuremberg Race Laws, later Adenauer's most powerful and influential Secretary of State. Compare Jürgen Bevers's *Der Mann hinter Adenauer – Hans Globkes Aufstieg vom NS-Juristen zur Grauen Eminenz der Bonner Repblik* (Berlin, 2009). Likewise, the TV documentary of the same name by Bevers and Pflechtinger, broadcast on *ARTE* on 8 October 2008.

The memoir of Inge Deutschkron is a worthwhile document about disenfranchisement, persecution, deportation and death, as well as illegality and loss of identity. It was published under the title *Ich trug den gelben Stern* (Munich, 1992). A sequel was published under the title *Mein Leben nach dem Überleben* (Munich, 2000).

The 'Honorable' Gentleman from Marburg
How a military judge made a career after 1945

Schwinge's significance in the context of the history of Nazi military justice is based on two publications. His *Kommentar zum Militärgesetzbuch,* published in Berlin as early as 1936 (6th edition 1944), was considered the standard commentary on Nazi military justice. His other work, edited and introduced by Otto Peter Schweling, is *Die deutsche Militärjustiz in der Zeit des Nationalsozialismus* (2nd edition, Marburg, 1978). The private researcher Fritz Wüllner, together with the historian Manfred Messerschmidt, wrote the book *Die Wehrmachtjustiz im Dienst des Nationalsozialismus – Zerstörung einer Legende* (Baden-Baden, 1987) against this history-blundering justification. It attracted a great deal of attention and triggered fierce attacks from the "whitewashers" of Nazi military historians such as Schwinge.

Fritz Wüllner called his work *Die NS-Militärjustiz und das Elend der Geschichtsschreibung* (Baden-Baden, 1991), a "fundamental research report". The fact-rich investigation refuted the manipulated figures and arguments of Schwinge's Nazi military history based on numerous documents. The actual number of trials that took place before Nazi military courts is still the subject of fierce controversy today. Schwinge mentions 700,000, Wüllner about 3 million and also includes trials of civilians in occupied territories, as well as trials of prisoners of war. The fact is that the German Nazi military justice system took particularly harsh action against the accused, and nearly 30,000 death sentences (Wüllner, 1991, p.90) proves this.

Also worth reading is Detlev Garbe's *"In jedem Einzelfall. . . bis zur Todesstrafe" – Der Militärstrafrechtler Erich Schwinge. Ein deutsches Juristenleben* (Hamburg, 1989), published in the "Small Historical Library" of the Hamburg Foundation for Social History of the Twentieth Century. Also, see *Kampfanzug unter der Robe – Kriegsgerichtsbarkeit des Zweiten und Dritte Weltkrieges* (Hamburg, 1984), by Ulrich Vultejus.

Schwinge's view of Germany's past and his political world view can be read in his book *Bilanz der Kriegsgeneration* (Marburg, 1979). The quoted review by Georg Geismann was published on Amazon on 12 April 2013.

The quotation from the foreword of Schwinge's *Der Staatsmann – Anspruch und Wirklichkeit* (Munich, 1983) can be found on p.9. Schwinge's essay *"Die Behandlung der Psychopathen im Militärstrafrecht"* is published in the *Zeitschrift für Wehrrecht*, Vol. 4, 1939/40, pp.110-25 (here on p.120). The death sentences against the soldiers Sorge and Tesch, excerpts of which are quoted here, can be found in Wüllner, 1991, pp.66–9. In his book, Wüllner documents further death sentences that Schwinge either demanded as a prosecutor or imposed as a judge.

Schwinge's book *Bundeswehr und Wehrmacht – Zum Problem der Traditionswürdigkeit* was published in Bonn in 1991 by the publishing house Soldat im Volk. The two quotations used can be found on p.35 and p.74.

Schwinge unleashed a series of lawsuits against his critics and opponents. The information on the court disputes mentioned here can be found in the essay *"Schwinge und seine Art von Vergangenheitsbewältigung"* in *Jura ALSO*, the newspaper of the law student council at Philipps University of Marburg an der Lahn, Winter 1991/1992, p.14.

The continuity of Nazi Wehrmacht justice and the work of former Wehrmacht lawyers after 1945, particularly their consequences for the "democratic" legal system, are addressed in the volume *Mit reinem Gewissen – Wehrmachtsrichter in der Bundesrepublik und ihre Opfer*, edited by Joachim Perels and Wolfram Wette (Berlin, 2011).

Schwinge's case is not the only example that shows how a Nazi past was by no means an obstacle to a post-war academic career. His immediate successor as rector of Philipps University of Marburg, the psychiatrist Proffessor Werner Villinger, also had a very "German" career. Formerly a Nazi physician who had taken part in forced sterilization procedures, he later appeared, among other things, as an expert in the Reparations Committee of the German Bundestag. Wolfram Schäfer provides a factual inventory of Werner Villinger and his exemplary career in *"Bis endlich der langersehnte Um-schwung kam.. . Anmerkungen zur Rolle des Marburger Psychiaters Werner Villinger in der NS- und Nachkriegszeit"*. The work is accompanied by further contributions in the anthology *"Bis endlich der langersehnte Umschwung kam. . ." – Von der Verantwortung der Medizin unter dem Nationalsozialismus*, published by the medical department of Philipps University of Marburg (Marburg an der Lahn, 1991, pp.178-283).

Reference should be made to a landmark ruling by the Federal Social Court in Kassel on 11 September 1991, which received little attention in the media. For the first time, the widows and children of deserters executed by the Nazi military justice system were also granted a pension. This ruling marked a turning point in German post-war jurisprudence. "In principle," according to the court, "the death sentences of the Wehrmacht courts are clearly unlawful." This verdict was a long time coming. Many survivors of "deserters", "morale destroyers" and "objectors" did not live to see the turning point and were never compensated. The late – yet necessary – verdict was mainly due to a different assessment of the German military courts, and the investigations by Manfred Messerschmidt and Fritz Wüllner played a decisive role in this. See also the report *"Der Terror der deutschen Militärgerichte im Weltkrieg"* by Otto Gritschneder in the *Süddeutsche Zeitung*, 1/2 February 1992, p.11.

The commemorative publication for Erich Schwinge on his 70th birthday, entitled *Persönlichkeit und Demokratie*, edited by Hans Ulrich Evers, Karl Heinrich Friauf, Ernst Walter Hanack and Rudolf Reinhardt, was published by Hanstein in Bonn, 1973.

"There has to be an end at some point"
The neighbor: a concentration camp murderer

Günther Schwarberg, a reporter at *Stern* for twenty years and author of numerous books on the history of the Third Reich, researched Arnold Strippel's concentration camp career like no other and brought it to the public's attention. All information concerning Arnold Strippel's CV, as well as the testimonies and excerpts from court rulings, are taken from his two books *Der SS-Arzt und die Kinder vom Bullenhuser Damm* (Göttingen, 1988) and *Der Juwelier von Majdanek* (Göttingen, 1991).

Walter Poller's report can be found in his book *Arztschreiber in Buchenwald* (Hamburg, 1946, p.136). You can read State Secretary Hermsdorf's answer from questions in the German Bundestag in *Verhandlungen des Deutschen Bundestages*, 7th electoral term, 29th session, Wednesday, 9 May 1963, *Stenographische Berichte*, Volume 81, p.1424.

Günther Schwarberg's impressions of the Majdanek trial are taken from his commentary *"Der Kreuzworträtsellöser"*, which was published in the Frankfurt magazine *Prinz*, No.10, October 1990, p.49.

A Death Sentence
or: The second career of Roland Freisler

The conversation with Frau Margot Diestel took place in February 1991 at her house in Steinhorst. The quoted book *Gerettetes Leben – Erinnerung an eine Jugend in Deutschland* was published in 1988 under her maiden name, Margot von Schade, by Langen Müller (Munich). A facsimile of the judgment of the People's Court against Margot von Schade is reproduced on pp.179-185.

A detailed documentation of the investigations of the public prosecutor's office at the Berlin Regional Court against former judges and prosecutors at the People's Court can be found in the brochure *Der Volksgerichtshof* by Bernhard Jahntz and Volker Kähne (Berlin, 1986).

For the termination of the investigation, see also Rolf Lamprecht's *"Die Gewalttäter in den Roten Roben"*, *DER SPIEGEL*, No. 44, 27 October 1986, pp.35-7, as well as the essay *"Ein Ende ohne Schrecken – Die Mörder des nationalsozialistischen Volksgegerichtshofes werde nicht zur Rechenschaftgt: Sie waren nur Richter an einem deutschen Gericht"* by Walter Boehlich, in *KONKRET*, No.12, December 1986, pp.30-2.

Judgments by the People's Court can be found in the book *"Im Namen des deutschen Volkes!" Todesurteile des Volksgerichtshofs*, edited by Heinz Hillermeier (Darmstadt und Neuwied, 1980). The verdict against Georg Jurkowski can be found at http://www.zeit.de/1987/20/im-namen-des-deutschen-volkes/complete view.

The most precise information on the origin, legal practice and internal structure of the People's Court can be found in the standard work *Der Volksgerichtshof im nationalsozialistischen Staat* by Walter Wagner (Stuttgart, 1974), as well as in an equally readable and informative book by Hannsjoachim W. Koch, *Volksgericht – Politische Justiz im 3. Reich* (Munich, 1988).

For information on Roland Freisler, including his career, work, and the sentencing practices of the People's Court, see Helmut Ortner's *Der Hinrichter: Roland Freisler – Mörder im Dienste Hitlers* (Frankfurt am Main, 2014).

Freisler's quoted article on the task of the People's Court appeared under the title *"Der Volksgerichtshof – das Reichsstrafgericht"* in *Zeitschrift der Akademie für Deutsches Recht*, Vol.2, 1935, pp.90-4.

His visions of a "Germanic court case" can be read in his essay *"Viel vom werdenden deutschen Blutbanngericht"* in *Deutsche Juristen-Zeitung*, Vol.40, 1935, col.584-96 and col.649-55.

A report on the atonement trial on 30 January 1958 was published in the *Süddeutsche Zeitung*. The author of this book has a copy of the judgment of 29 January 1958, with the file number "Sprkn 7/56". Press reports on the pension case of Freisler's widow appeared in all major German daily newspapers, including the *Süddeutsche Zeitung*, 13 February to 19 February 1985, *DER SPIEGEL*, 18 February, and the *Frankfurter Rundschau*, 13 and 18 February 1985.

The Man at the Guillotine
A German executioner's life

The text was first published under the title *"Der Mann am Fallbeil: Johann Reichhart – Ein deutsches Henkersleben"*, in *Das Buch vom Töten – Über die Todesstrafe* by Helmut Ortner, Spring 2013, p.112-34.

Josef Dachs describes the life and work of the executioner Johann Reichhart in his book *Tod durch das Fallbeil – Der deutsche Scharfrichter Johann Reichhart (1803-1972)* (Regensburg, 1996).

The Forgotten Heroes
Resistance fighters Georg Elser and Maurice Bavaud

The article first appeared under the title *"Dreizehn Minuten"* at the start of the film *Elser – Er hätte die Welt verändert* (April, 2015), directed by Oliver Hirschbiegel, *www.faustkultur.de*.

A historical comparison of Georg Elser and Count von Stauffenberg can be found in *"Der Mann, der Hitler töten wollen"* by Helmut Ortner in *Cicero – Magazin für politische Kultur*, No.11, November 2009, pp.72-3.

For Georg Elser's life story, the plans and preparation for his assassination attempt, his arrest and interrogation, and finally his imprisonment and murder, see the comprehensive *Der einsame Attentäter – Georg Elser, der Mann der Hitler töten wollte* by Helmut Ortner (Darmstadt, 2013).

For the debate surrounding the artist's competition in connection with a monument to Georg Elser in Berlin, see the press release of the Berlin Senate Chancellery of 12 October 2011, as well as numerous press reports, including *"Georg Elser-Denkmal in Berlin"* at www.spiegel-online/kultur.de and *"Denkmal für einen tragischen Helden"* at www.süddeutsche.de.

For criticism on a homogeneous culture of remembrance, which is also evident in the person of Georg Elser, see, among others, *"Mythos Elser"* by Peter Koblanz at www.georg-elser-arbeitskreise.de. All schools, squares and streets in Germany named after Georg Elser are also listed there.

The life and death of Maurice Bavaud is vividly described by Niklaus Meienberg in *Es ist kalt in Brandenburg – Ein Hitler-Attentat* (Berlin, 1990). Rolf Hochhuth also pays tribute to Bavaud in his book *Tell '38* (Reinbek, 1979).

The Führer Lives
or: Hitler as a media pop star

From an insider tip to a million-copy bestseller, and translated into numerous languages, see the novel *Er ist wieder da* by Timur Vermes (Cologne, 2012).

The book tells the following story: Adolf Hitler wakes up in the summer of 2011 in a vacant property in Berlin-Mitte. Without a war, without a party, without Eva, but surrounded by thousands of foreigners and Angela Merkel. Sixty-six years after his supposed end, against all odds he starts a new career on television. This Hitler, however, is not a joke figure, but frighteningly real. The country he encounters, the Federal Republic of Germany, the so-called cosmopolitan "Berlin Republic", is cynical and unrestrainedly greedy for success, and has no chance against a population addicted to ratings and "likes".

The novel – and the film of the same name, released in October 2015 and directed by David Wendt – triggered both applause and debate. Was it a pastiche? Satire? A political comedy? Or all of them together?

Compare also the conversation between the author Timur Vermes and the Nazi historian Axel Drecoll about how a "resurrected Hitler" could become so popular again today and how corruptible Germany still is, *DIE ZEIT*, 8 October 2015, p.20.

Adolf Hitler: Mein Kampf. A critical edition, commissioned by the Institute of Contemporary History by Christian Hartmann, Thomas Vordermayer, Othmar Plöckinger and Roman Töppel (Munich and Berlin, 2016).

For the debate surrounding this edition, see the article *"Das Monstrum"* by Martin Doerry and Klaus Wiegrefe in *DER SPIEGEL*, No.2, 9 January 2016, pp.106-15. See also Jeremy Adler's *"Das absolute Böse"* in the *Süddeutsche Zeitung*, 7 January 2016, p.9. Sven Felix Kellerhoff's *Mein Kampf – Die Karriere eines deutschen Buches* (Stuttgart, 2015), and Rolf Rietzler's *Mensch Adolf – Das Hitler-Bild der Deutschen seit 1945* (Munich, 2016) are also worth reading.

BIBLIOGRAPHY

Bevers, Jürgen, *Der Mann hinter Adenauer: Hans Globkes Aufstieg vom NS-Juristen zur Grauen Eminenz der Bonner Republik* (Berlin: Links, 2009).

Browning, Christoper R., *Ganz normale Männer. Das Reservebataillon 101 und die "Endlösung" in Polen* (Reinbek: Rowohlt-Taschenbuch-Verlag, 1996).

Conze, Eckhart / Frei, Norbert / Hayes, Peter / Zimmermann, Moshe, *Deutsche Diplomaten im Dritten Reich und in der Bundesrepublik* (Munich: Blessing, 2010).

Dachs, Josef, *Tod durch das Fallbeil: Der deutsche Scharfrichter Johann Reichhart (1893–1972)* (Regensburg: Mittelbayerische Druck- und Verlagsgesellschaft, 1996).

Deutschkron, Inge, *Ich trug den gelben Stern* (München: Deutscher Taschenbuch-Verlag, 1992).

Deutschkron, Inge, *Mein Leben nach dem Überleben* (Munich: Deutscher Taschenbuch-Verlag, 2000).

Fachschaft Medizin der Philipps-Universität Marburg (ed.), *"Bis endlich der langersehnte Umschwung kam. . .", Verantwortung der Medizin unter dem Nationalsozialismus* (Marburg an der Lahn: Schüren, 1991).

Frei, Norbert (ed.), *Hitlers Eliten nach 1945* (Munich: Deutscher Taschenbuch-Verlag, 2003).

Frei, Norbert, *1945 und wir: Das Dritte Reich im Bewußtsein der Deutschen* (Munich: Beck, 2005).

Friedrich, Jörg, *Die kalte Amnestie: NS-Täter in der Bundesrepublik* (Frankfurt am Main: Fischer-Taschenbuch-Verlag, 1988).

Fritzsche, Peter, *Wie aus Deutschen Nazis wurden* (Zürich: Pendo, 1999).

Garbe, Detlef, *"In jedem Einzelfall... bis zur Todesstrafe". Der Militärstrafrechtler Erich Schwinge: Ein deutsches Juristenleben* (Hamburg: Hamburger Stiftung für Sozialgeschichte, 1989).

Giordano, Ralph, *Die zweite Schuld oder Von der Last, Deutscher zu sein* (Hamburg: Rasch und Röhring, 1987).

Heer, Hannes, *"Hitlers war's!" Die Befreiung der Deutschen vor ihrer Vergangenheit* (Berlin: Aufbau-Verlag, 2005).

Hilberg, Raul, *Anatomie des Holocaust: Essays und Erinnerungen*, edited by Walter H. Pehle and René Schlott (Frankfurt am Main: S. Fischer, 2016).

Hilberg, Raul, *Die Vernichtung der europäischen Juden. Die Gesamtgeschichte des Holocaust* (Berlin: Olle und Wolter, 1982).

Hillermeier, Heinz (Ed.), *"Im Namen des deutschen Volkes!" Todesurteile des Volksgerichtshofs* (Darmstadt und Neuwied: Luchterhand, 1980).

Hitler, Adolf, *Mein Kampf: Eine kritische Edition*, edited by Christian Hartmann, Thomas Vordermayer, Othmar Plöckinger and Roman Töppel on behalf of the Munich Institute for Contemporary History (Munich and Berlin: Institute of Contemporary History, 2016).

Hochhuth, Rolf, *Tell '38* (Reinbek: Rowohlt, 1979).

Jahntz, Bernhard / Kähne, Volker, *Der Volksgerichtshof. Darstellung der Ermittlungen der Staatsanwaltschaft bei dem Landgericht Berlin gegen ehemalige Richter und Staatsanwälte am Volksgerichtshof* (Berlin: Senator für Justiz und Bundesangelegenheiten, 1986).

Kellerhoff, Sven Felix, *"Mein Kampf": Die Karriere eines deutschen Buches* (Stuttgart: Klett-Cotta, 2015).

Kershaw, Ian, *Das Ende: Kampf bis in den Untergang – NS-Deutschland 1944/45* (Munich: Deutsche Verlags-Anstalt, 2011).

Kershaw, Ian, *Der NS-Staat: Geschichtsinterpretationen und Kontroversen im Überblick* (Reinbek: Rowohlt, 1988).

Klee, Ernst, *Das Personenlexikon zum Dritten Reich. Wer was vor und nach 1945 war* (Frankfurt am Main: Fischer-Taschenbuch-Verlag, 2015).

Koch, Hannsjoachim W., *Volksgerichtshof: Politische Justiz im 3. Reich* (Munich: Universitas-Verlag, 1988).

Marszałek, Józef, *Majdanek: Konzentrationslager Lublin* (Warsaw: Verlag Interpress, 1984).

Meienberg, Niklaus, *Es ist kalt in Brandenburg: Ein Hitler Attentat* (Berlin: Wagenbach, 1990).

Messerschmidt, Manfred / Wüllner, Fritz, *Die Wehrmachtjustiz in Dienst des Nationalsozialismus. Zerstörung einer Legende* (Baden-Baden: Nomos-Verlagsgesellschaft, 1987).

Mitscherlich, Alexander / Mitscherlich, Margarete, *Die Unfähigkeit zu trauern: Grundlagen kollektiven Verhaltens* (Munich: Piper, 1967).

Ortner, Helmut, *Das Buch vom Töten: Über die Todesstrafe* (Springe: ze Klampen, 2013).

Ortner, Helmut, *Der einsame Attentäter: Georg Elser – der Mann der Hitler töten wollte* (Darmstadt: Wissenschaftliche Buchgemeinschaft, 2013).

Ortner, Helmut, *Der Hinrichter. Roland Freisler – Mörder im Dienste Hitlers* (revised edition) (Frankfurt am Main: Nomen-Verlag, 2014).

Ortner, Helmut (ed.), *Hitlers Schatten – Aktuelle Reportagen* (Frankfurt am Main: Nomen-Verlag, 2009).

Pauen, Michael / Welzer, Harald, *Autonomie – Eine Verteidigung* (Frankfurt am Main: S. Fischer, 2015).

Perels, Joachim / Wette, Wolfram (eds.), *Mit reinem Gewissen. Wehrmachtsrichter in der Bundesrepublik und ihre Opfer* (Berlin: Aufbau-Verlag, 2011).

Poller, Walter, *Arztschreiber in Buchenwald. Bericht des Häftlings 996 aus Block 39* (Hamburg: Phönix-Verlag, 1946).

Rietzler, Rolf, *Mensch Adolf – Das Hitler-Bild der Deutschen seit 1945* (Munich: Bertelsmann, 2016).

Schade, Margot von, *Gerettetes Leben: Erinnerung an eine Jugend in Deutschland* (Munich: Langen Müller, 1988).

Schlink, Bernhard, *Vergangenheitsschuld: Beiträge zu einem deutschen Thema* (Zurich: Diogenes, 2007).

Schwarberg, Günther, *Der Juwelier von Majdanek* (Göttingen: Steidl, 1991).

Schwarberg, Günther, *Der SS-Arzt und die Kinder vom Bullenhuser Damm* (Göttingen: Steidl, 1988).

Schwinge, Erich, *Bilanz der Kriegsgeneration. Ein Beitrag zur Geschichte unserer Zeit* (Marburg an der Lahn: Elwert, 1979).

Schwinge, Erich, *Bundeswehr und Wehrmacht. Zum Problem der Traditionswürdigkeit* (Bonn: Verlag Soldat im Volk, 1991).

Schwinge, Erich, *Verfälschung und Wahrheit. Das Bild der Wehrmachtgerichtsbarkeit* (Tübingen, Zurich and Paris: Hohenrain-Verlag, 1988).

Steinke, Ronen, *Fritz Bauer oder Auschwitz vor Gericht* (Munich and Zurich: Piper, 2013).

Ullrich, Christina, *"Ich fühl mich nicht als Mörder!" Die Integration von NS-Tätern in die Nachkriegsgesellschaft* (Darmstadt: Wissenschaftliche Buchgemeinschaft, 2011).

Vermes, Timur, *Er ist wieder da* (Cologne: Eichhorn, 2012).

Vultejus, Ulrich, *Kampfanzug unter der Robe: Kriegsgerichtsbarkeit des Zweiten und Dritten Weltkrieges* (Hamburg: Buntbuch-Verlag, 1984).

Wagner, Walter, *Der Volksgerichtshof im nationalsozialistischen Staat* (Stuttgart: Deutsche Verlags-Anstalt, 1974).

Welzer, Harald, *Täter: Wie aus ganz normalen Menschen Massenmörder werden* (Frankfurt am Main: S. Fischer, 2005).

Wüllner, Fritz, *Die NS-Militärjustiz und das Elend der Geschichtsschreibung: Ein grundlegender Forschungsbericht* (Baden-Baden: Nomos-Verlagsgesellschaft, 1991).

OTHER BOOKS BY HELMUT ORTNER

Fremde Feinde
Sacco und Vanzetti – Ein Justizmord
Hardcover, 296pp. 24,90 Euro
ISBN 978-3-939816-25-6
Also available as an e-book

Widerstand ist zwecklos. Aber sinnvoll
Notwehr-Notizen von der Heimat-Front
Softcover, 200pp. 19,90 Euro
ISBN 978-3-939816-19-5
Also available as an e-book

Der Hinrchter
Roland Freisler – Mörder im Dienst Hitlers
Hardback, 360pp. 24,90 Euro
ISBN 978-3-939816-21-8
Accompanies the widely acclaimed TV documentary "Roland Freisler
 – Hitlers williger Vollstrecker" (ARD).

Der einsame Attentäter
Georg Elser – Der Mann, der Hitler töten wollen
Hardcover, 240pp. 16,90 Euro
ISBN 978-3-939816-03-4

Hitlers Schatten
Hardcover, 160pp. 19,90 Euro
ISBN 978-3-939816-16-4

Täter. Opfer. Komplizen
*Kassette mit 4 Bänden: Der Hinrichter. Der einsame Attentäter. Hitlers
Schatten. Täter, Opfer, Komplizen – Rezensionen und Reflexionen*
Bound, 832pp. 49.90 Euro
ISBN 978-3-939816-15-7

Falsche Wahrheiten, Richtige Lügen
*Täter, Opfer, Zuschauer. Über deutsche Vergangenheitsbewältigung:
Reportagen, Recherchen, Berichte*
Softcover, 104pp. 12,00 Euro
ISBN 978-3-9809981-0-9

Alles andere später
*Attacken, Notizen und Kolumnen zum Stand der Dinge und Lauf der
Zeit*
Softcover, 196pp.16,00 Euro
ISBN 978-3-9809981-1-6

Nomen Verlag Homburger Landstraße 105 60435 Frankfurt
am Main Phone: 069 / 95 41 62 13
fax: 069 / 95 41 62 14
E-mail: nomen@nomen-verlag.de

INDEX